THE FOOD PROCESSOR COOKBOOK

pil

Publications International, Ltd.

Some of the products listed in this publication may be in limited distribution.

Photo on front cover and page 95 © shutterstock.com

Pictured on the back cover *(clockwise from top right):* Strawberry Fields Salad *(page 120),* St. Patty's Pops *(page 152),* and Chorizo-Potato Hash with Crisp Crumb Topping *(page 32).*

ISBN: 978-1-64030-446-8

Manufactured in China.

8 7 6 5 4 3 2 1

Microwave Cooking: Microwave ovens vary in wattage. Use the cooking times as guidelines and check for doneness before adding more time.

TABLE OF CONTENTS

APPETIZERS & DIPS

SALSA

Makes 4½ cups

---

1 can (28 ounces) whole Italian plum tomatoes, undrained

2 fresh plum tomatoes, seeded and coarsely chopped

2 tablespoons canned diced mild green chiles

1 tablespoon canned diced jalapeño peppers (optional)

1 tablespoon white vinegar

1 clove garlic, minced

1 teaspoon onion powder

1 teaspoon sugar

1 teaspoon ground cumin

½ teaspoon garlic powder

¼ teaspoon salt

Combine tomatoes with juice, fresh tomatoes, green chiles, jalapeño peppers, if desired, vinegar, garlic, onion powder, sugar, cumin, garlic powder and salt in food processor; process until finely chopped.

ROASTED EGGPLANT HUMMUS

Makes about 1½ cups

1 large eggplant (about 1½ pounds)

1 clove garlic

¼ cup tahini (sesame paste)

Salt and black pepper

1. Preheat oven to 400°F. Line small baking sheet with foil.

2. Place eggplant on baking sheet; roast about 1 hour or until soft. When cool enough to handle, remove and discard skin.

3. Combine garlic, roasted eggplant and tahini in food processor; process until smooth. Season with salt and pepper to taste.

TIPS: Serve with pita bread wedges or toasted pita chips. For extra flavor, stir 2 tablespoons fresh lemon juice into the hummus before serving.

ROASTED RED PEPPER DIP

Makes about 2½ cups

2 cups crumbled feta cheese

2 tablespoons garlic-flavored olive oil

¼ teaspoon black pepper

1 jar (12 ounces) roasted red pepper strips, drained

Pita chips or cut-up vegetables

1. Process cheese, oil and black pepper in food processor 1 minute or until smooth.

2. Add red peppers. Process 10 to 15 seconds or until mixed but not puréed. Serve with pita chips or vegetables.

OLIVE TAPENADE

Makes 1¾ cups

1 can (6 ounces) medium pitted black olives

½ cup pimiento-stuffed green olives

1 tablespoon roasted garlic*

½ teaspoon dry mustard

½ cup (2 ounces) crumbled feta cheese

1 tablespoon olive oil

Toast slices

To roast garlic, preheat oven to 400°F. Remove outer layers of papery skin and cut ¼ inch off top of garlic head. Place cut side up on a piece of heavy-duty foil. Drizzle with 2 teaspoons olive oil; wrap tightly in foil. Bake 25 to 30 minutes or until cloves feel soft when pressed. Cool slightly before squeezing out garlic pulp.

1. Process olives, roasted garlic and mustard in food processor until finely chopped.

2. Combine olive mixture, feta cheese and oil in medium bowl; stir until well blended. Serve with toast slices.

TIP: For the best flavor, prepare this tapenade several hours or 1 day ahead to allow the flavors to blend.

QUICK AND EASY STUFFED MUSHROOMS

Makes 8 servings

1 slice whole wheat bread

16 large mushrooms

½ cup sliced celery

½ cup sliced onion

1 clove garlic

1 teaspoon Worcestershire sauce

½ teaspoon marjoram leaves, crushed

⅛ teaspoon ground red pepper

Dash paprika

1. Tear bread into pieces; place in food processor. Process 30 seconds or until crumbs are formed. Transfer to small bowl; set aside.

2. Remove stems from mushrooms; reserve caps. Place mushroom stems, celery, onion and garlic in food processor; process using on/off pulses until vegetables are finely chopped.

3. Spray large skillet with nonstick cooking spray. Add vegetable mixture; cook and stir over medium heat 5 minutes or until onion is tender. Remove to bowl. Stir in bread crumbs, Worcestershire sauce, marjoram and red pepper.

4. Fill mushroom caps evenly with mixture, pressing down firmly. Place about ½ inch apart in shallow baking pan. Spray tops with nonstick cooking spray. Sprinkle with paprika.

5. Preheat oven to 350°F. Bake 15 minutes or until heated through.

NOTE: Mushrooms can be stuffed up to 1 day ahead. Refrigerate filled mushroom caps, covered, until ready to serve. Bake in preheated 300°F oven 20 minutes or until heated through.

RAMEN HUMMUS

Makes about 2⅓ cups

1 package (3 ounces) chicken-flavored ramen noodles

1 can (about 15 ounces) chickpeas, rinsed and drained

¼ cup chopped fresh basil

1 medium clove garlic, minced

½ cup water

¼ cup extra virgin olive oil

3 tablespoons fresh lemon juice

⅛ teaspoon ground red pepper

¼ teaspoon salt

Fresh vegetable slices or pita chips

1. Prepare noodles according to package directions, cooking on high heat for 5 minutes instead of recommended 3 minutes. Rinse and drain under cool running water.

2. Combine noodles, ramen seasoning packet, chickpeas, basil, garlic, water, oil, lemon juice, ground red pepper and salt in food processor; process until smooth, scraping down sides occasionally. Cover and refrigerate at least 1 hour before serving.

3. Serve with fresh vegetables or pita chips.

TIP: By adding the noodles to this hummus recipe, you stretch the quantity of the recipe. You'll get more volume for less!

AVOCADO EGG ROLLS

Makes 8 to 10 servings (20 pieces) and 1 cup sauce

DIPPING SAUCE

½ cup cashew nut pieces

½ cup packed fresh cilantro

¼ cup honey

2 green onions, coarsely chopped

2 cloves garlic

1 tablespoon white vinegar

1 teaspoon balsamic vinegar

1 teaspoon ground cumin

½ teaspoon tamarind paste

⅛ teaspoon ground turmeric

¼ cup olive oil

EGG ROLLS

2 avocados, peeled and pitted

¼ cup chopped drained oil-packed sun-dried tomatoes

2 tablespoons diced red onion

2 tablespoons chopped fresh cilantro

1 tablespoon lime juice

¼ teaspoon salt

10 egg roll wrappers

Vegetable oil for frying

1. For sauce, combine cashews, cilantro, honey, green onions, garlic, white vinegar, balsamic vinegar, cumin, tamarind paste and turmeric in food processor; process until coarsely chopped. With motor running, drizzle in olive oil in thin steady stream; process until finely chopped and well blended. Refrigerate until ready to use.

2. For egg rolls, place avocados in medium bowl; coarsely mash with potato masher. Stir in sun-dried tomatoes, red onion, chopped cilantro, lime juice and salt until well blended.

3. Working with one at a time, place egg roll wrapper on work surface with one corner facing you. Spread 2 tablespoons filling horizontally across wrapper. Fold short sides over filling and fold up bottom corner over filling. Moisten top edges with water; roll up egg roll, pressing to seal. Refrigerate until ready to cook.

4. Heat 2 inches of vegetable oil in large saucepan over medium-high heat to 350°F; adjust heat to maintain temperature. Cook egg rolls in batches about 3 minutes or until golden brown, turning once. Drain on paper towel-lined plate. Cut egg rolls in half diagonally; serve with sauce.

TEX-MEX GUACAMOLE PLATTER

Makes 6 to 8 servings

4   ripe avocados

¼   cup fresh lime juice

2   tablespoons olive oil

3   cloves garlic, crushed

½   teaspoon salt

¼   teaspoon black pepper

1   cup (4 ounces) shredded
    Colby Jack cheese

1   cup diced seeded plum
    tomatoes

⅓   cup sliced pitted black
    olives

⅓   cup salsa

1   tablespoon minced fresh
    cilantro

    Tortilla chips

1. Cut avocados in half; remove pits. Scoop out pulp into food processor. Add lime juice, oil, garlic, salt and pepper. Cover; process until almost smooth.

2. Spread avocado mixture evenly on large dinner plate or serving platter, leaving border around edge. Top with cheese, tomatoes, olives, salsa and cilantro. Serve with tortilla chips.

SWIMMING TUNA DIP

Makes 4 servings

1 cup low-fat (1%) cottage cheese

1 tablespoon reduced-fat mayonnaise

1 tablespoon lemon juice

2 teaspoons dry ranch-style salad dressing mix

1 can (3 ounces) chunk white tuna packed in water, drained and flaked

2 tablespoons sliced green onion or chopped celery

1 teaspoon dried parsley flakes

1 package (12 ounces) peeled baby carrots

1. Combine cottage cheese, mayonnaise, lemon juice and salad dressing mix in food processor. Cover and process until smooth.

2. Combine tuna, green onion and parsley flakes in small bowl. Stir in cottage cheese mixture. Serve with carrots.

LAVASH CHIPS WITH ARTICHOKE PESTO

Makes about 1½ cups

3 pieces lavash bread, each 7½×9½ inches

¼ cup plus 2 tablespoons olive oil, divided

¾ teaspoon kosher salt, divided

1 can (14 ounces) artichoke hearts, rinsed and drained

½ cup chopped walnuts, toasted*

¼ cup packed fresh basil leaves

1 clove garlic, minced

2 tablespoons lemon juice

¼ cup grated Parmesan cheese

*To toast walnuts, spread on baking sheet. Bake in preheated 350°F oven 6 to 8 minutes or until golden brown, stirring frequently.

1. Preheat oven to 350°F. Line two baking sheets with parchment paper. Position two oven racks in upper third and lower third of oven.

2. Brush both sides of each piece lavash with 2 tablespoons oil. Sprinkle with ¼ teaspoon salt. Bake 10 minutes or until lavash is crisp and browned, turning and rotating baking sheets between upper and lower racks after 5 minutes. Remove from oven; set on wire rack to cool completely.

3. Place artichoke hearts, walnuts, basil, garlic, lemon juice and remaining ½ teaspoon salt in food processor; pulse about 12 times until coarsely chopped. While food processor is running, slowly stream remaining ¼ cup oil until smooth. Add cheese and pulse until blended.

4. Break lavash into chips. Serve with pesto.

BREAKFAST & BRUNCH

SPICY MEXICAN FRITTATA

Makes 4 servings

1 fresh jalapeño pepper*

1 clove garlic

1 medium tomato, peeled, quartered and seeded

½ teaspoon ground coriander

½ teaspoon chili powder

½ cup chopped onion

1 cup frozen corn

6 egg whites

2 eggs

¼ cup fat-free (skim) milk

¼ teaspoon salt

¼ teaspoon black pepper

¼ cup (1 ounce) shredded part-skim farmer or mozzarella cheese

Jalapeño peppers can sting and irritate the skin, so wear rubber gloves when handling peppers and do not touch your eyes.

1. Place jalapeño pepper and garlic in food processor; process until finely chopped. Add tomato, coriander and chili powder. Cover; process until tomato is almost smooth.

2. Spray large skillet with nonstick cooking spray; heat over medium heat. Add onion; cook and stir 5 minutes or until tender. Stir in tomato mixture and corn; cook 3 to 4 minutes or until liquid is almost evaporated, stirring occasionally.

3. Combine egg whites, eggs, milk, salt and black pepper in medium bowl. Add egg mixture all at once to skillet. Cook, without stirring, 2 minutes or until eggs begin to set. Run large spoon around edge of skillet, lifting eggs for even cooking. Remove skillet from heat when eggs are almost set but surface is still moist.

4. Sprinkle with cheese. Cover; let stand 3 to 4 minutes or until surface is set and cheese is melted. Cut into four wedges.

QUINOA PANCAKES
WITH TOMATO CHUTNEY

Makes 5 servings

TOMATO CHUTNEY

 1   tablespoon vegetable oil

 ½   teaspoon cumin seeds

 ½   onion, finely chopped

 2   cloves garlic, finely chopped

 2   teaspoons grated fresh ginger

 2   cups tomatoes, seeded and chopped

 1   green chile, seeded and chopped (optional)

 1   teaspoon ground coriander

 1   teaspoon salt

 2   teaspoons sugar

PANCAKES

 1   cup buttermilk pancake mix

 1   cup red quinoa, cooked and cooled

 1   egg, beaten

 1¼ cups fat-free (skim) milk

 1   cup spinach, finely chopped

1. For chutney, heat oil in small skillet over medium heat. Add cumin seeds; cook several seconds until seeds stop popping. Add onion, garlic and ginger; cook and stir 1 to 2 minutes or until onions are translucent. Add tomatoes, green chile, coriander and salt; cook 3 to 4 minutes until tomatoes are soft, stirring occasionally. Stir in sugar. Set aside 5 to 10 minutes to cool.

2. Add chutney to food processor; pulse until chutney has uniformly coarse texture. Serve immediately or cover and refrigerate. (Chutney will keep in refrigerator up to 1 week.)

3. For pancakes, combine pancake mix and quinoa in medium bowl; mix well. Stir in egg and milk until blended. Fold in spinach. Let stand 10 minutes.

4. Spray medium skillet with nonstick cooking spray; heat over medium heat. Pour ¼ cup batter into skillet for each pancake; cook until tops are bubbled and the bottoms are lightly browned. Turn pancakes; cook 1 minute. Serve warm with Tomato Chutney.

CHEESE BLINTZES

Makes about 8 servings

1¼ cups milk

1 cup all-purpose flour

3 eggs

1 tablespoon cornstarch

½ teaspoon salt

3 tablespoons plus
   1 teaspoon butter or
   margarine, divided

1 container (15 ounces)
   ricotta cheese

2 packages (3 ounces each)
   cream cheese, softened

3 tablespoons sugar

¼ teaspoon almond extract

   Fruit pie filling, fresh fruit
   or frozen fruit, thawed

   Sour cream (optional)

1. Combine milk, flour, eggs, cornstarch and salt in food processor; process just until smooth. Pour into 1-quart glass measure; set aside.

2. Melt ½ teaspoon butter in medium skillet over medium heat. Pour about 3 tablespoons batter into bottom of skillet, swirling to cover bottom. Cook 1 to 2 minutes or until bottom is browned.

3. Invert blintz onto large plate. Rub butter over browned surface.

4. Repeat steps 2 and 3 with remaining batter, stacking and buttering cooked blintzes on plate.

5. Beat ricotta cheese, cream cheese, sugar and almond extract in large bowl with electric mixer at medium speed just until blended.

6. Place 2 tablespoons filling in center on unbrowned side of each blintz. Fold in sides about 1 inch; fold in opposite edges to enclose filling and form rectangular shape.

7. Melt ½ tablespoon butter in large skillet over medium heat. Add blintzes in batches and cook 2 minutes per side, until heated through. top with fruit pie filling and sour cream, if desired.

MUSHROOM & ONION EGG BAKE

Makes about 6 servings

1 tablespoon vegetable oil

4 ounces sliced mushrooms

4 green onions, chopped

1 cup low-fat (1%) cottage cheese

6 eggs

1 cup sour cream

2 tablespoons all-purpose flour

¼ teaspoon salt

⅛ teaspoon black pepper

Dash hot pepper sauce

1. Preheat oven to 350°F. Spray shallow 1-quart baking dish with nonstick cooking spray.

2. Heat oil in medium skillet over medium heat. Add mushrooms and green onions; cook and stir until tender.

3. Place cottage cheese in food processor; process until almost smooth. Add eggs, sour cream, flour, salt, black pepper and hot pepper sauce; process until blended. Stir in mushrooms and green onions. Pour into prepared baking dish.

4. Bake 40 minutes or until knife inserted near center comes out clean.

CHORIZO-POTATO HASH
WITH CRISP CRUMB TOPPING

Makes 6 servings

1 naan bread, torn into uneven pieces

6 tablespoons plus 1 teaspoon olive oil, divided

Kosher salt and black pepper

1 pound Mexican chorizo, casings removed

1 onion, diced

1 yellow bell pepper, diced

1 red bell pepper, diced

2 Russet potatoes, peeled, shredded, rinsed and squeezed dry *or* 1 bag (1 pound 4 ounces) refrigerated shredded hash brown potatoes

1 green onion, sliced on the bias

1. Place naan pieces in food processor; pulse until small crumbs form, about 15 pulses. Transfer to large bowl; toss with 2 tablespoons oil.

2. Heat large skillet over medium heat. Add crumbs; cook 6 to 8 minutes or until browned and toasted, stirring occasionally. Season with salt and black pepper; set aside.

3. Heat 1 teaspoon oil in same skillet over medium-high heat. Add chorizo; cook about 5 minutes or until browned, using spatula to break up the meat. Transfer to paper towel-lined plate. Heat 1 tablespoon oil in same skillet; add onion and bell peppers; cook about 8 minutes or until tender, stirring occasionally. Season with salt and black pepper. Transfer to bowl.

4. Heat remaining 3 tablespoons oil in same skillet; add potatoes in even layer; cook about 3 minutes or until browned and beginning to crisp on bottom. Turn potatoes, continue to cook about 10 minutes or until tender and evenly browned, stirring occasionally. Season with salt and black pepper. Stir in chorizo and onion-bell pepper mixture; cook 2 minutes until heated through. Top with bread crumbs and green onion.

TIP: This recipe is especially good to make when you have day-old or stale flatbread.

ROASTED PEPPER AND SOURDOUGH BRUNCH CASSEROLE

Makes 8 servings

3 cups sourdough bread cubes

1 jar (12 ounces) roasted red pepper strips, drained

1 cup (4 ounces) shredded reduced-fat sharp Cheddar cheese

1 cup (4 ounces) shredded reduced-fat Monterey Jack cheese

1 cup fat-free cottage cheese

1½ cups cholesterol-free egg substitute

1 cup fat-free (skim) milk

¼ cup chopped fresh cilantro

¼ teaspoon black pepper

SLOW COOKER DIRECTIONS

1. Coat slow cooker with nonstick cooking spray. Add bread. Arrange roasted peppers evenly over bread cubes; sprinkle with Cheddar and Monterey Jack cheeses.

2. Place cottage cheese in food processor; process until smooth. Add egg substitute and milk; process just until blended. Stir in cilantro and black pepper. Pour over ingredients in slow cooker.

3. Cover; cook on LOW 3 to 3½ hours or on HIGH 2 to 2½ hours until eggs are firm but still moist. Adjust seasonings, if desired.

STRAWBERRY CRÊPES

Makes 8 to 10 crêpes

1 cup whipping cream

1 package (16 ounces) frozen sweetened sliced strawberries, thawed, divided

1 package (5 ounces) crêpes (10 crêpes)

1. Beat cream in large chilled bowl with electric mixer at high speed until stiff peaks form.

2. Chop half of strawberries; stir into whipped cream. Spoon about 2 tablespoons of mixture down center of each crêpe and roll up. Cover; refrigerate until ready to serve.

3. Process remaining strawberries in food processor until smooth. Drizzle over crêpes.

BERRY BUCKWHEAT SCONES

Makes 8 scones

1¼ cups all-purpose flour

¾ cup buckwheat flour, plus additional for dusting

¼ cup packed light brown sugar

1 tablespoon baking powder

½ teaspoon salt

½ cup (1 stick) cold unsalted butter, cut into 8 pieces

¾ cup fresh raspberries

¾ cup fresh blackberries

1 egg

½ cup whipping cream

1 tablespoon granulated sugar

Jam or lemon curd (optional)

1. Preheat oven to 375°F. Line baking sheet with parchment paper.

2. Combine all-purpose flour, ¾ cup buckwheat flour, brown sugar, baking powder and salt in bowl of food processor; pulse until combined. Add butter; pulse until pea-sized pieces of butter remain. Transfer mixture to large bowl; stir in berries.

3. Whisk egg and cream in small bowl. Stir cream mixture into flour mixture until soft dough forms.

4. Transfer dough to work surface lightly dusted with buckwheat flour; gently pat into an 8-inch round about ¾ inches thick. Cut into eight equal wedges.

5. Place wedges 1½ inches apart on prepared baking sheet. Sprinkle tops with granulated sugar. Bake 20 to 25 minutes or until golden. Transfer to wire rack; cool 10 minutes before serving.

6. Serve with jam or lemon curd, if desired.

SWEET POTATO LATKES
WITH CRANBERRY COMPOTE

Makes 7 servings

CRANBERRY COMPOTE

1½   cups fresh cranberries

    Peel of 1 orange

½   cinnamon stick

4   peppercorns, cracked

2   whole cloves

½   cup orange juice

¼   cup brandy

⅛   cup packed brown sugar

¼   cup water

LATKES

1   pound uncooked sweet
    potatoes

2   eggs

¼   cup all-purpose flour

1   small leek, thinly sliced
    (white part only)

    Salt and black pepper to
    taste

¼   cup matzo meal

¼   cup canola oil

1. For compote, place all ingredients in saucepan over medium-low heat; cook about 25 minutes or until cranberries pop and liquid is slightly reduced. Set aside.

2. For latkes, peel potatoes and shred using food processor. Place all ingredients except oil in large bowl and using your hands (a spoon will break up the potato), combine until ingredients are equally distributed.

3. Heat oil in large frying pan over high heat until very hot but not smoking. Flatten about 2 tablespoons batter into pancakes with your hands and gently place in oil. Cook latkes about 2 minutes per side or until browned. Gently remove from oil and place on paper towels to drain.

4. Serve with Cranberry Compote spooned on top of pancakes.

MEXICAN OMELET ROLL-UPS WITH AVOCADO SAUCE

Makes 8 servings

2 cups cholesterol-free egg substitute

2 tablespoons 2% milk

1 tablespoon margarine

1½ cups (6 ounces) shredded Monterey Jack cheese

1 large tomato, seeded and chopped

¼ cup chopped fresh cilantro

8 corn tortillas

2 medium avocados, chopped

¼ cup reduced-fat sour cream

2 tablespoons finely chopped onion

1 jalapeño or serrano pepper,* chopped (optional)

1 to 2 teaspoons lime juice

¼ teaspoon salt

¼ teaspoon minced garlic

*Jalapeño peppers can sting and irritate the skin, so wear rubber gloves when handling peppers and do not touch your eyes.

1. Preheat oven to 350°F. Spray 13X9-inch baking dish with nonstick cooking spray.

2. Whisk egg substitute and milk in medium bowl until blended. Melt margarine in large skillet over medium heat. Add egg mixture; cook and stir 5 minutes or until eggs are set, but still soft. Remove from heat. Stir in cheese, tomato and cilantro.

3. Spoon about ⅓ cup egg mixture evenly down center of each tortilla. Roll up tortillas and place seam side down in prepared dish.

4. Cover tightly with foil and bake 20 minutes or until heated through.

5. Meanwhile, process avocados, sour cream, onion, jalapeño pepper, lime juice, salt and garlic in food processor until smooth. Serve roll-ups with avocado sauce.

SOUPS & CHOWDERS

SWEET POTATO BISQUE

Makes 4 servings

1 pound sweet potatoes, peeled and cut into 2-inch chunks

2 teaspoons butter

½ cup finely chopped onion

1 teaspoon curry powder

½ teaspoon ground coriander

¼ teaspoon salt

⅔ cup unsweetened apple juice

1 cup buttermilk

¼ cup water (optional)

Fresh snipped chives (optional)

Plain nonfat yogurt (optional)

1. Place sweet potatoes in large saucepan; cover with water. Bring to a boil over high heat. Cook 15 minutes or until potatoes are fork-tender. Drain; cool under cold running water.

2. Meanwhile, melt butter in small saucepan over medium heat. Add onion; cook and stir 2 minutes. Stir in curry powder, coriander and salt; cook and stir 1 minute or until onion is tender. Remove from heat; stir in apple juice.

3. Combine sweet potatoes, buttermilk and onion mixture in food processor; cover and process until smooth. Return to saucepan; stir in ¼ cup water, if necessary, to thin to desired consistency. Cook and stir over medium heat until heated through. *Do not boil.* Garnish with chives and/or dollop of yogurt.

CORN AND JALAPEÑO CHOWDER

Makes 4 servings

4 cups frozen whole-kernel corn, thawed, divided

2 cups reduced-sodium chicken broth, divided

2 jalapeño peppers,* seeded and finely chopped

¼ teaspoon onion salt

1½ teaspoons whole cumin seeds, crushed

1 cup fat-free half-and-half

4 tablespoons (1 ounce) shredded reduced-fat Cheddar cheese, divided

4 tablespoons thinly sliced roasted red pepper, divided

Jalapeño peppers can sting and irritate the skin, so wear rubber gloves when handling peppers and do not touch your eyes.

1. Combine 2 cups corn and 1 cup broth in food processor. Cover; process until nearly smooth.

2. Stir together blended corn mixture, remaining corn, remaining broth, jalapeño peppers, onion salt and cumin seeds in large saucepan. Bring to a boil. Reduce heat. Cover; simmer 5 minutes.

3. Stir in half-and-half. Heat through. Sprinkle each serving with 1 tablespoon cheese and 1 tablespoon red pepper.

GAZPACHO

Makes 6 servings

2 large cucumbers, peeled, seeded, divided

12 plum tomatoes, seeded, divided

1 cup chopped yellow or green bell pepper, divided

⅓ cup green onions, sliced, divided

1 cup reduced-sodium chicken broth

½ cup reduced-sodium vegetable juice cocktail

½ teaspoon dried thyme, crushed

3 tablespoons red wine vinegar

¼ to ½ teaspoon hot pepper sauce

1 can (2¼ ounces) sliced black olives

3 tablespoons crumbled feta cheese (optional)

2 teaspoons drained capers (optional)

6 breadsticks or whole wheat rolls

1. Chop 1 cucumber and 10 tomatoes. Combine chopped cucumber, chopped tomatoes, ½ cup bell pepper, 2 tablespoons green onions, broth, vegetable juice and thyme in food processor; process until puréed (if necessary, process in 2 batches). Skim foam from juice. Add vinegar and hot pepper sauce.

2. Chop remaining cucumber and 2 tomatoes. Combine with remaining ½ cup bell pepper and green onions. Add vegetables to puréed mixture. Cover and chill thoroughly 2 hours or up to 24 hours. Top with olives. Garnish with cheese and capers, if desired. Serve with breadsticks or whole wheat rolls.

CHICKEN AND CORN CHOWDER

Makes 4 servings

1 tablespoon olive oil

1 pound boneless skinless
   chicken breasts, cut into
   ½-inch pieces

3 cups thawed frozen corn

¾ cup coarsely chopped
   onion (about 1 medium)

1 to 2 tablespoons water

1 cup diced carrots

2 tablespoons finely
   chopped jalapeño
   pepper* (optional)

½ teaspoon dried oregano

¼ teaspoon dried thyme

3 cups reduced-sodium
   chicken broth

1½ cups milk

½ teaspoon salt

*Jalapeño peppers can sting and
irritate the skin, so wear rubber
gloves when handling peppers
and do not touch your eyes.*

1. Heat oil in large nonstick saucepan over medium heat. Add chicken; cook and stir about 10 minutes or until browned and no longer pink in center. Remove chicken.

2. Add corn and onion to saucepan; cook and stir about 5 minutes or until onion is tender. Place 1 cup corn mixture in food processor. Process until finely chopped, adding water to liquify mixture; reserve.

3. Add carrots, jalapeño pepper, if desired, oregano and thyme to saucepan; cook and stir about 5 minutes or until corn begins to brown. Return chicken to saucepan. Stir in broth, milk, chopped corn mixture and salt; bring to a boil. Reduce heat to low; cover and simmer 15 to 20 minutes.

TWO-CHEESE POTATO
AND CAULIFLOWER SOUP

Makes 4 to 6 servings

1 tablespoon butter

1 cup chopped onion

2 cloves garlic, minced

5 cups whole milk

1 pound Yukon Gold potatoes, peeled and diced

1 pound cauliflower florets

1½ teaspoons salt

⅛ teaspoon ground red pepper

1½ cups (6 ounces) shredded sharp Cheddar cheese

⅓ cup crumbled blue cheese

1. Melt butter in large saucepan over medium-high heat. Add onion; cook and stir 4 minutes or until translucent. Add garlic; cook and stir 15 seconds. Add milk, potatoes, cauliflower, salt and red pepper; bring to a boil. Reduce heat to low. Cover tightly and simmer 15 minutes or until potatoes are tender. Cool slightly.

2. Working in batches, process soup in food processor until smooth. Return to saucepan. Cook and stir over medium heat just until heated through. Remove from heat; stir in cheeses until melted.

TIP: One pound of trimmed cauliflower will yield about 1½ cups of florets. You can also substitute 1 pound of frozen cauliflower florets for the fresh florets.

CHILLED CANTALOUPE SOUP

Makes 4 servings

½ medium to large cantaloupe, rind removed, seeded and cut into cubes

¼ cup plain nonfat Greek yogurt

¾ cup half-and-half

Salt and white pepper

Slivered cantaloupe (optional)

1. Place cubed cantaloupe in food processor; process until smooth. Add yogurt; process until blended.

2. Pour cantaloupe mixture into medium bowl; stir in half-and-half. Season with salt and pepper to taste. Refrigerate until ready to serve. Garnish with slivered cantaloupe.

SUMMER HONEYDEW SOUP: Substitute ½ medium honeydew melon for cantaloupe.

TIP: This refreshing soup makes a great first course, light lunch or breakfast.

BLACK BEAN SOUP

Makes 4 to 6 servings

2   tablespoons vegetable oil

1   cup diced onion

1   stalk celery, diced

2   carrots, diced

½   small green bell pepper, diced

4   cloves garlic, minced

4   cans (15 ounces each) black beans, rinsed and drained, divided

4   cups (32 ounces) chicken or vegetable broth, divided

2   tablespoons cider vinegar

2   teaspoons chili powder

½   teaspoon salt

½   teaspoon ground red pepper

½   teaspoon ground cumin

¼   teaspoon liquid smoke

Garnishes: sour cream, chopped green onions and shredded Cheddar cheese

1. Heat oil in large saucepan or Dutch oven over medium-low heat. Add onion, celery, carrots, bell pepper and garlic; cook 10 minutes, stirring occasionally.

2. Combine half of beans and 1 cup broth in food processor; process until smooth. Add to vegetables in saucepan.

3. Stir in remaining beans, broth, vinegar, chili powder, salt, red pepper, cumin and liquid smoke; bring to a boil over high heat. Reduce heat to medium-low; cook 1 hour or until vegetables are tender and soup is thickened. Garnish as desired.

BROCCOLI CHEESE SOUP

Makes 4 to 6 servings

6 tablespoons (¾ stick) butter

1 cup chopped onion

1 clove garlic, minced

¼ cup all-purpose flour

2 cups vegetable broth

2 cups milk

1½ teaspoons Dijon mustard

½ teaspoon salt

¼ teaspoon ground nutmeg

¼ teaspoon black pepper

⅛ teaspoon hot pepper sauce

1 package (16 ounces) frozen broccoli (5 cups)

2 carrots, shredded (1 cup)

6 ounces pasteurized process cheese product, cubed

1 cup (4 ounces) shredded sharp Cheddar cheese, plus additional for garnish

1. Melt butter in large saucepan or Dutch oven over medium-low heat. Add onion; cook and stir 10 minutes or until softened. Add garlic; cook and stir 1 minute. Increase heat to medium. Whisk in flour until smooth; cook and stir 3 minutes without browning.

2. Gradually whisk in broth and milk. Add mustard, salt, nutmeg, black pepper and hot pepper sauce; cook 15 minutes or until thickened.

3. Add broccoli; cook 15 minutes. Add carrots; cook 10 minutes or until vegetables are tender.

4. Transfer half of soup to food processor; process until smooth. Return to saucepan. Add cheese product and 1 cup Cheddar; cook and stir over low heat until cheese is melted. Ladle into bowls; garnish with additional Cheddar.

MOLE CHILI

Makes 4 to 6 servings

2 corn tortillas, each cut into 4 wedges

1½ pounds boneless beef chuck, cut into 1-inch pieces

¾ teaspoon salt

½ teaspoon ground black pepper

3 tablespoons olive oil, divided

2 medium onions, chopped

5 cloves garlic, minced

1 cup beef broth

1 can (about 14 ounces) fire roasted diced tomatoes

2 tablespoons chili powder

1 tablespoon ground ancho chile

1 teaspoon ground cumin

1 teaspoon dried oregano

¾ teaspoon ground cinnamon

1 can (about 15 ounces) red kidney beans, rinsed and drained

1½ ounces semisweet chocolate, chopped

Queso fresco and chopped fresh cilantro (optional)

SLOW COOKER DIRECTIONS

1. Coat inside of slow cooker with nonstick cooking spray. Place tortillas in food processor; process to fine crumbs. Set aside.

2. Season beef with salt and pepper. Heat 1 tablespoon oil in large skillet over medium-high heat. Add half of beef to skillet; cook 4 minutes or until browned. Remove to slow cooker. Repeat with remaining 1 tablespoon oil and beef.

3. Heat remaining 1 tablespoon oil in skillet. Add onions and garlic; cook 2 minutes or until starting to soften. Pour broth into skillet, scraping up any browned bits from bottom of skillet. Remove to slow cooker. Stir in reserved tortilla crumbs, tomatoes, chili powder, ancho chile, cumin, oregano and cinnamon.

4. Cover; cook on LOW 8 to 8½ hours. Stir in beans. Cover; cook on LOW 30 minutes. Turn off heat. Stir in chocolate until melted. Top with queso fresco and cilantro, if desired.

HARVEST PUMPKIN SOUP

Makes 8 servings

1 sugar pumpkin or acorn
  squash (about 2 pounds)

1 kabocha or butternut
  squash (about 2 pounds)

Salt and black pepper

2 tablespoons olive oil

2 tablespoons butter

1 large onion, finely chopped
  (about 1¾ cups)

1 medium carrot, chopped
  (½ cup)

2 stalks celery, chopped
  (½ cup)

¼ cup packed brown sugar

2 tablespoons tomato paste

1 tablespoon minced fresh
  ginger

1 clove garlic, minced

1 teaspoon salt

1 teaspoon ground cinnamon

¼ teaspoon ground cumin

¼ teaspoon black pepper

4 cups vegetable broth

1 cup milk

2 teaspoons lemon juice

Roasted pumpkin seeds
  (optional, see Tip)

1. Preheat oven to 400°F. Line large baking sheet with foil; spray with nonstick cooking spray.

2. Cut pumpkin and kabocha squash in half; scoop out seeds and strings. Season cut sides with salt and pepper. Place cut sides down on large baking sheet; bake 30 to 45 minutes or until fork-tender. When squash is cool enough to handle, remove skin; chop flesh into 1-inch pieces.

3. Heat oil and butter in large saucepan over medium-high heat. Add onion, carrot and celery; cook and stir 5 minutes or until vegetables are tender. Add brown sugar, tomato paste, ginger, garlic, 1 teaspoon salt, cinnamon, cumin and ¼ teaspoon pepper; cook and stir 1 minute. Add broth and squash; bring to a boil. Reduce heat to medium; cook 20 minutes or until squash is very soft.

4. Process soup in batches in food processor. Stir in milk and lemon juice; heat through. Garnish with pumpkin seeds.

TIP: Roasted pumpkin seeds can be found at many supermarkets, or you can roast the seeds that you remove from the pumpkin and squash in the recipe. Combine the seeds with 2 teaspoons vegetable oil and ⅛ teaspoon salt in a small bowl; toss to coat. Spread in a single layer on a small foil-lined baking sheet; bake at 300°F 20 to 25 minutes or until the seeds begin to brown, stirring once.

CREAMY TOMATO SOUP

Makes 6 servings

3 tablespoons olive oil, divided

2 tablespoons butter

1 large onion, finely chopped

2 cloves garlic, minced

2 teaspoons sugar

1 teaspoon salt

½ teaspoon dried oregano

2 cans (28 ounces each) peeled Italian plum tomatoes, undrained

4 cups ½-inch focaccia cubes (half of 9-ounce loaf)

½ teaspoon freshly ground black pepper

½ cup whipping cream

1. Heat 2 tablespoons oil and butter in large saucepan over medium-high heat. Add onion; cook and stir 5 minutes or until softened. Add garlic, sugar, salt and oregano; cook 30 seconds. Add tomatoes with juice; bring to a boil. Reduce heat to medium-low; simmer 45 minutes, stirring occasionally.

2. Meanwhile, prepare croutons. Preheat oven to 350°F. Combine focaccia cubes, remaining 1 tablespoon oil and pepper in large bowl; toss to coat. Spread on large rimmed baking sheet. Bake about 10 minutes or until bread cubes are golden brown.

3. Process soup in food processor. Stir in cream; heat through. Serve soup topped with croutons.

CREAMY CAULIFLOWER BISQUE

Makes 9 servings

1 pound frozen cauliflower florets, thawed

1 pound russet potatoes, peeled and cut into 1-inch cubes

2 cans (about 14 ounces each) fat-free reduced-sodium chicken broth

1 cup chopped yellow onion

½ teaspoon dried thyme

¼ teaspoon garlic powder

⅛ teaspoon ground red pepper

1 cup fat-free evaporated milk

2 tablespoons butter

½ teaspoon salt

¼ teaspoon black pepper

1 cup (4 ounces) shredded reduced-fat sharp Cheddar cheese

¼ cup finely chopped fresh parsley

¼ cup finely chopped green onions

SLOW COOKER DIRECTIONS

1. Layer cauliflower, potatoes, broth, onion, thyme, garlic powder and red pepper in 4-quart slow cooker. Cover; cook on LOW 8 hours or on HIGH 4 hours.

2. Working in batches, process soup in food processor until smooth; return to slow cooker. Add evaporated milk, butter, salt and black pepper. Cook, uncovered, on HIGH 30 minutes or until heated through.

3. Ladle into bowls. Top each serving with cheese, parsley and green onions.

MAIN DISHES

CILANTRO-STUFFED CHICKEN BREASTS

Makes 4 servings

2 cloves garlic

1 cup packed fresh cilantro leaves

1 tablespoon plus 2 teaspoons soy sauce, divided

1 tablespoon peanut or vegetable oil

4 boneless chicken breasts (about 1¼ pounds)

1 tablespoon dark sesame oil

1. Preheat oven to 350°F. Mince garlic in food processor. Add cilantro; process until cilantro is minced. Add 2 teaspoons soy sauce and peanut oil; process until paste forms.

2. With rubber spatula or fingers, distribute about 1 tablespoon cilantro mixture evenly under skin of each chicken breast, taking care not to puncture skin.

3. Place chicken on rack in shallow, foil-lined baking pan. Combine remaining 1 tablespoon soy sauce and sesame oil in small bowl. Brush half of mixture evenly over chicken. Bake 25 minutes; brush remaining soy sauce mixture evenly over chicken. Bake 10 minutes or until juices run clear.

LINGUINE WITH SUN-DRIED TOMATO PESTO

Makes 4 servings

½ cup sun-dried tomatoes

½ cup loosely packed fresh
    basil leaves

2 tablespoons olive oil

1½ tablespoons grated
    Parmesan cheese

1 teaspoon dried oregano

1 clove garlic, minced

8 ounces linguine or angel
    hair pasta, cooked and
    kept warm

1. Combine sun-dried tomatoes with ½ cup hot water in small bowl; soak 3 to 5 minutes or until tomatoes are soft and pliable. Drain; reserve liquid.

2. Combine tomatoes, basil, oil, cheese, oregano and garlic in food processor. Process, adding enough reserved liquid, until mixture is of medium to thick sauce consistency. Spoon over pasta and toss to coat; serve immediately.

TUNA NOODLE CASSEROLE

Makes 6 servings

8 ounces uncooked wide cholesterol-free whole wheat egg noodles

½ cup finely chopped onion

1 can (10 ounces) reduced-fat condensed cream of mushroom soup, undiluted

½ cup reduced-fat sour cream

½ cup low-fat (1%) milk

⅛ teaspoon ground red pepper

12 ounces white tuna packed in water, drained and broken into chunks

1½ cups frozen baby peas

1 slice whole wheat or multigrain bread

½ teaspoon paprika

1. Preheat oven to 350°F. Spray 2½-quart casserole with nonstick cooking spray. Cook noodles according to package directions, omitting salt and fat. Drain; return to saucepan.

2. Meanwhile, spray large skillet with cooking spray. Add onion; cook and stir over medium heat 4 to 5 minutes or until tender. Stir in soup, sour cream, milk and red pepper until well blended. Add soup mixture, tuna and peas to noodles. Toss well; transfer mixture to prepared casserole.

3. Tear bread into pieces; place in bowl of food processor. Process until finely ground. Sprinkle evenly over casserole; top with paprika.

4. Bake 30 to 35 minutes or until heated through.

PESTO-STUFFED GRILLED CHICKEN

Makes 6 servings

2 cloves garlic, peeled

½ cup packed fresh basil leaves

2 tablespoons pine nuts or walnuts, toasted*

¼ teaspoon black pepper

5 tablespoons extra virgin olive oil, divided

¼ cup grated Parmesan cheese

1 fresh or thawed frozen roasting chicken or capon (6 to 7 pounds)

2 tablespoons fresh lemon juice

Additional fresh basil leaves and fresh red currants (optional)

To toast pine nuts, spread in single layer on baking sheet. Bake in preheated 350°F oven 8 to 10 minutes or until golden brown, stirring frequently.

1. Prepare grill with rectangular metal or foil drip pan. Bank briquettes on either side of drip pan for indirect cooking.

2. Meanwhile, to prepare pesto, drop garlic through feed tube of food processor with motor running. Add ½ cup basil, pine nuts and black pepper; process until basil is minced. With processor running, add 3 tablespoons oil in slow, steady stream until smooth paste forms, scraping down side of bowl once. Add cheese; process until well blended.

3. Remove giblets from chicken cavity; reserve for another use. Loosen skin over breast of chicken by pushing fingers between skin and meat, taking care not to tear skin. Do not loosen skin over wings and drumsticks. Using rubber spatula or small spoon, spread pesto under breast skin; massage skin to evenly spread pesto. Combine remaining 2 tablespoons oil and lemon juice in small bowl; brush over chicken skin. Insert meat thermometer into center of thickest part of thigh, not touching bone. Tuck wings under back; tie legs together with kitchen string.

4. Place chicken, breast side up, on grid directly over drip pan. Grill, on covered grill, over medium-low coals 1 hour 10 minutes to 1 hour 30 minutes or until thermometer registers 185°F, adding 4 to 9 briquettes to both sides of the fire after 45 minutes to maintain medium-low coals. Transfer chicken to carving board; tent with foil. Let stand 15 minutes before carving. Garnish with additional basil and currants.

CLASSIC PESTO WITH LINGUINE

Makes 4 servings

12 ounces uncooked linguine

2 tablespoons butter

¼ cup plus 1 tablespoon olive oil, divided

2 tablespoons pine nuts

1 cup tightly packed fresh basil leaves

2 cloves garlic

¼ teaspoon salt

¼ cup grated Parmesan cheese

1½ tablespoons grated Romano cheese

1. Cook linguine according to package directions; drain. Toss with butter in large serving bowl; set aside and keep warm.

2. Meanwhile, heat 1 tablespoon oil in small skillet over medium-low heat. Add pine nuts; cook and stir 30 to 45 seconds until light brown, shaking pan constantly. Remove with slotted spoon; drain on paper towels.

3. Place toasted pine nuts, basil, garlic and salt in food processor. With processor running, add remaining ¼ cup oil in slow, steady stream; process until evenly blended and pine nuts are finely chopped.

4. Transfer basil mixture to small bowl. Stir in Parmesan and Romano cheeses.*

5. Add pesto sauce to pasta; toss until well coated. Serve immediately.

*Pesto sauce can be stored at this point in an airtight container; pour thin layer of olive oil over pesto and cover. Refrigerate up to 1 week. Bring to room temperature before using. Proceed as directed in step 5.

PINEAPPLE-HOISIN HENS

Makes 4 servings

2 cloves garlic

1 can (8 ounces) crushed pineapple in juice, undrained

2 tablespoons rice vinegar

2 tablespoons soy sauce

2 tablespoons hoisin sauce

2 teaspoons minced fresh ginger

1 teaspoon Chinese five-spice powder*

2 large Cornish hens (about 1½ pounds each), split in half

Chinese five-spice powder consists of cinnamon, cloves, fennel seed, star anise and Szechuan peppercorns. It can be found at Asian markets and in most supermarkets.

1. Mince garlic in food processor. Add pineapple with juice; process until fairly smooth. Add remaining ingredients except hens; process 5 seconds.

2. Place hens in large resealable food storage bag; pour pineapple mixture over hens. Seal bag; turn to coat. Marinate in refrigerator at least 2 hours or up to 24 hours, turning bag once.

3. Preheat oven to 375°F. Drain hens; reserve marinade. Place hens, skin side up, on rack in shallow, foil-lined roasting pan. Roast 35 minutes.

4. Brush hens lightly with some reserved marinade; discard remaining marinade. Roast 10 minutes or until hens are browned and cooked through (180°F).

LENTIL BURGERS

Makes 4 servings

1   can (about 14 ounces) vegetable broth

1   cup dried lentils, rinsed and sorted

1   small carrot, grated

¼   cup coarsely chopped mushrooms

1   egg

¼   cup plain dry bread crumbs

3   tablespoons finely chopped onion

2   to 4 cloves garlic, minced

1   teaspoon dried thyme

¼   cup plain fat-free yogurt

¼   cup chopped seeded cucumber

½   teaspoon dried mint

¼   teaspoon dried dill weed

¼   teaspoon black pepper

⅛   teaspoon salt

     Dash hot pepper sauce (optional)

     Kaiser rolls (optional)

1. Bring broth to a boil in medium saucepan over high heat. Stir in lentils; reduce heat to low. Simmer, covered, about 30 minutes or until lentils are tender and liquid is absorbed. Cool to room temperature.

2. Place lentils, carrot and mushrooms in food processor; process until finely chopped but not smooth. (Some whole lentils should still be visible.) Stir in egg, bread crumbs, onion, garlic and thyme. Refrigerate, covered, 2 to 3 hours.

3. Shape lentil mixture into four (½-inch-thick) patties. Spray large skillet with nonstick cooking spray; heat over medium heat. Cook patties over medium-low heat about 10 minutes or until browned on both sides.

4. Meanwhile, for sauce, combine yogurt, cucumber, mint, dill, black pepper, salt and hot pepper sauce, if desired, in small bowl. Serve burgers on rolls with sauce.

CHICKEN WITH HERB STUFFING

Makes 4 servings

⅓ cup fresh basil leaves

1 package (8 ounces) goat cheese with garlic and herbs

4 boneless skinless chicken breasts

1 to 2 tablespoons olive oil

1. Place basil in food processor; process using on/off pulsing action until chopped. Cut goat cheese into large pieces and add to food processor; process using on/off pulsing action until combined.

2. Preheat oven to 350°F. Place 1 chicken breast on cutting board and cover with plastic wrap. Pound with meat mallet until ¼ inch thick. Repeat with remaining chicken.

3. Shape about 2 tablespoons of cheese mixture into log and set in center of each chicken breast. Wrap chicken around filling to enclose completely. Tie securely with kitchen string.

4. Heat 1 tablespoon oil in large ovenproof skillet; brown chicken bundles on all sides, adding additional oil as needed to prevent sticking. Place skillet in oven; bake 15 minutes or until chicken is cooked through and filling is hot. Allow to cool slightly, remove string and slice to serve.

SPICED CHICKEN SKEWERS
WITH YOGURT-TAHINI SAUCE

Makes 8 servings

1 cup plain nonfat Greek yogurt

¼ cup chopped fresh parsley, plus additional for garnish

¼ cup tahini*

2 tablespoons lemon juice

1 clove garlic

¾ teaspoon salt, divided

1 tablespoon vegetable oil

2 teaspoons garam masala**

1 pound boneless skinless chicken breasts, cut into 1-inch pieces

Tahini, a thick paste made from ground sesame seeds, is available in the international foods section of major supermarkets, Middle Eastern markets or health food stores.

**Garam masala is a blend of Indian spices available in the spice aisle of many supermarkets. If garam masala is unavailable, substitute 1 teaspoon each ground cumin and ground coriander.*

1. Spray grill grid with nonstick cooking spray. Prepare grill for direct cooking.

2. For yogurt-tahini sauce, combine yogurt, ¼ cup parsley, tahini, lemon juice, garlic and ¼ teaspoon salt in food processor; process until combined. Set aside.

3. Combine oil, garam masala and remaining ½ teaspoon salt in medium bowl. Add chicken; toss to coat evenly. Thread chicken on eight (6-inch) wooden or metal or skewers.***

4. Grill chicken skewers over medium-high heat 5 minutes per side or until chicken is no longer pink. Serve with yogurt-tahini sauce. Garnish with additional parsley.

***If using wooden skewers, soak in cold water 30 minutes to prevent burning.*

SUMMER'S BOUNTY PASTA WITH BROCCOLI PESTO

Makes 4 servings

2 cups broccoli florets

2 cups uncooked farfalle (bowtie pasta)

½ cup loosely packed fresh basil leaves

5 tablespoons shredded Parmesan-Romano cheese blend, divided

2 tablespoons chopped walnuts, toasted*

1½ tablespoons extra virgin olive oil

2 cloves garlic, crushed and divided

⅛ teaspoon salt

6 ounces medium cooked shrimp

¼ teaspoon black pepper

1 package (6 ounces) fresh baby spinach

1 cup halved grape tomatoes

To toast walnuts, spread in heavy skillet. Cook over medium heat 1 to 2 minutes or until nuts are lightly browned, stirring frequently.

1. Bring large saucepan of water to a boil. Add broccoli; cook 3 minutes or until tender. Remove to small bowl with slotted spoon; reserve water.

2. Cook pasta according to package directions using reserved water, omitting salt. Drain pasta; cover to keep warm.

3. Combine broccoli, basil, 3 tablespoons cheese, walnuts, oil, 1 clove garlic and salt in food processor; process until smooth. Stir into pasta in saucepan; toss to coat. Cover to keep warm.

4. Spray large skillet with nonstick cooking spray; heat over medium heat. Add shrimp, remaining 1 clove garlic and pepper; cook and stir until heated through. Stir in spinach and tomatoes; cook until spinach is wilted and tomatoes begin to soften. Add to pasta; stir gently to combine.

5. Divide pasta mixture evenly among four serving bowls; top with remaining 2 tablespoons cheese.

APRICOT BRISKET

Makes 8 servings

1 cup chopped dried
    apricots, divided

1 cup canned diced
    tomatoes, divided

2 teaspoons ground cumin

1 teaspoon salt, divided

1 clove garlic

¼ teaspoon ground cinnamon

1 medium onion, thinly sliced

2 large carrots, cut into
    1-inch pieces

1 small beef brisket (about
    2 to 3 pounds), trimmed
    of fat

½ teaspoon black pepper

1½ cups low-sodium beef
    broth

2 tablespoons cold water

2 tablespoons cornstarch

Chopped fresh parsley
    (optional)

1. Preheat oven to 325°F.

2. Combine ½ cup chopped apricots, ½ cup tomatoes, cumin, ½ teaspoon salt, garlic and cinnamon in food processor. Process using on/off pulses until coarsely combined.

3. Place onion and carrots on bottom of roasting pan. Place brisket on top. Cut several small slits across top of brisket; gently spoon apricot mixture into slits. Sprinkle brisket with remaining ½ teaspoon salt and pepper. Spread remaining ½ cup diced tomatoes over brisket; top with remaining ½ cup apricots. Drizzle broth over brisket. Cover with foil.

4. Roast 2 to 2½ hours. Transfer brisket to carving board; tent with foil and let stand 15 minutes.

5. Pour pan juices and vegetables into medium saucepan. Stir water into cornstarch in small bowl until smooth and well blended. Stir into pan juices; simmer about 5 minutes or until thickened.

6. Carve brisket crosswise into thin slices; serve with onion, carrots, tomatoes, apricots and pan juices. Sprinkle with parsley, if desired.

CRAB CAKES

Makes 12 cakes

CRAB CAKES

- 1 package (3 ounces) shrimp-flavored ramen noodles
- 1 egg
- ¼ cup mayonnaise
- 1 tablespoon chopped fresh dill
- 2 teaspoons fresh lemon juice
- 1 pound fresh crabmeat, drained and picked
- 2 tablespoons butter
- 2 tablespoons olive oil

LEMON DILL DIPPING SAUCE

- ½ cup plain nonfat Greek yogurt
- Juice of 1 lemon
- 1 tablespoon olive oil
- 1 tablespoon chopped fresh dill
- ½ teaspoon salt

1. For crab cakes, process ramen noodles in food processor until crumbs form. Place crumbs in large bowl; add ramen seasoning packet, egg, mayonnaise, dill and lemon juice; stir well. Fold in crabmeat; refrigerate 1 hour.

2. Using hands, form mixture into 12 patties. Heat 1 tablespoon butter and 1 tablespoon oil in large nonstick skillet over medium-high heat. Cook six patties, 5 minutes per side, or until golden brown. Repeat with remaining butter, oil and crab mixture.

3. For dipping sauce, combine yogurt, lemon juice, oil, dill and salt in small bowl; stir well. Refrigerate until ready to serve. Serve crab cakes with dipping sauce.

PESTO FARRO SALAD
WITH PEAS, ASPARAGUS AND FETA

Makes 4 servings

1 cup uncooked pearled farro

1 cup peas

1 bunch asparagus, trimmed and cut into 1-inch pieces

2 cups packed fresh basil leaves

½ cup packed fresh Italian parsley

¼ cup toasted walnuts

2 cloves garlic

½ cup extra virgin olive oil

½ cup grated Parmesan cheese

Coarse salt and black pepper

½ cup crumbled feta cheese

1. Bring large saucepan of water to a boil over high heat. Add farro; reduce heat to medium-low. Cook about 30 minutes or until tender, adding peas during last 5 minutes of cooking time and asparagus during last 2 minutes of cooking time. Drain well.

2. Meanwhile, place basil, parsley, walnuts and garlic in food processor. Pulse until coarsely chopped. With motor running, add oil in thin, steady stream. Add Parmesan cheese; pulse to combine. Season with salt and pepper.

3. Transfer farro mixture to large bowl. Add ¾ cup pesto mixture; toss to coat. (Reserve remaining pesto for another use.) Add feta cheese; stir until combined. Season with additional salt and pepper, if desired.

RAVIOLI WITH PESTO AND PEAS

Makes 6 servings

2 packages (10 ounces each) fresh cheese ravioli

¾ cup frozen peas

¼ cup pine nuts

4 cloves garlic

2 cups packed fresh basil leaves, packed

½ teaspoon kosher salt

¼ teaspoon black pepper

¾ cup olive oil

¾ cup grated Parmesan cheese, divided

1. Prepare ravioli according to package directions. Add peas to ravioli during last minute of cooking. Drain and set aside.

2. Combine pine nuts and garlic in food processor; process 15 seconds. Add basil, salt and pepper. With motor running, slowly pour oil through feed tube and process until finely chopped. Add half of cheese, process 30 seconds.

3. Toss pesto with ravioli and peas. Garnish with remaining cheese.

QUINOA PATTIES WITH
ROASTED RED PEPPER SAUCE

Makes 6 servings

1 cup uncooked quinoa

2 cups water

1 jar (12 ounces) roasted red peppers, drained

1 tablespoon balsamic vinegar

1 teaspoon lemon juice

1 teaspoon sugar

1 clove garlic

4 eggs, beaten

½ teaspoon salt

⅓ cup grated Parmesan cheese

2 tablespoons chopped fresh parsley

2 cloves garlic, minced

1 cup Italian-style dry bread crumbs

1 to 2 tablespoons olive oil

1. Place quinoa in fine-mesh strainer; rinse well under cold running water.

2. Bring 2 cups water in medium saucepan to a boil over high heat; stir in quinoa. Reduce heat to low; cover and simmer 10 to 15 minutes or until quinoa is tender and water is absorbed. Cool slightly.

3. Meanwhile, process roasted peppers, vinegar, lemon juice, sugar and garlic clove in food processor until smooth. Set aside.

4. Combine quinoa, eggs, salt, cheese, parsley, minced garlic and bread crumbs in large bowl. Form into 12 (¼-cup) patties.

5. Heat 1 tablespoon oil in large skillet over medium heat. Add six patties; cook 5 to 7 minutes or until bottoms are browned. Flip patties; cook 5 to 7 minutes. Repeat with remaining patties, adding additional 1 tablespoon oil, if necessary.

6. Serve patties with red pepper sauce.

VARIATION: Make 24 mini quinoa patties as an appetizer.

ROASTED RED PEPPER, EGGPLANT, GOAT CHEESE AND OLIVE PIZZA

Makes 4 servings

1 small eggplant, cut into ¼-inch-thick slices

1 tablespoon olive oil

¼ cup finely chopped onion

1 tablespoon minced fresh rosemary leaves *or* 2 teaspoons dried rosemary

3 cloves garlic, minced

1 (12-inch) prepared pizza crust

½ cup roasted red pepper strips

2 ounces goat cheese, crumbled

6 kalamata olives, pitted and halved

Black pepper

1. Preheat oven to 500°F. Spray baking sheet with nonstick cooking spray. Place eggplant slices on baking sheet; spray with cooking spray. Bake 8 to 10 minutes or until light golden. Turn slices; bake 6 to 8 minutes or until golden and very tender. Set aside.

2. Meanwhile, heat oil in small skillet over medium heat. Cook and stir onion, rosemary and garlic 3 to 4 minutes or until onion is translucent; set aside.

3. Bake pizza crust 3 to 4 minutes or until top is crisp and beginning to brown.

4. Process roasted pepper strips in food processor until smooth; spread evenly over baked crust, leaving 1-inch border. Arrange eggplant on top, slightly overlapping slices; sprinkle with onion mixture. Top with cheese, olives and black pepper. Bake 3 to 5 minutes or until crust is deep golden.

PESTO CAVATAPPI

Makes 4 to 6 servings

PESTO

2 cups packed fresh basil
   leaves*

1 cup walnuts, toasted

½ cup shredded Parmesan
   cheese, plus additional
   for garnish

4 cloves garlic

1 teaspoon salt

¼ teaspoon black pepper

¾ cup extra virgin olive oil

PASTA

1 package (16 ounces)
   uncooked cavatappi
   pasta

1 tablespoon extra virgin
   olive oil

2 plum tomatoes, diced
   (1½ cups)

1 package (8 ounces) sliced
   mushrooms

¼ cup dry white wine

¼ cup vegetable broth

¼ cup whipping cream

*Or substitute 1 cup packed fresh
parsley for half of basil.*

1. For pesto, combine basil, walnuts, ½ cup cheese, garlic, salt and black pepper in food processor; pulse until coarsely chopped. With motor running, add ¾ cup oil in thin, steady stream; process until well blended. Measure 1 cup for pasta; reserve remaining pesto for another use.

2. Cook pasta in large saucepan of boiling salted water according to package directions until al dente. Drain and return to saucepan; keep warm.

3. Meanwhile, heat 1 tablespoon oil in large skillet over medium-high heat. Add tomatoes and mushrooms; cook about 7 minutes or until most of liquid has evaporated, stirring occasionally. Add wine, broth and cream; bring to a boil. Reduce heat to low; cook about 4 minutes or until sauce has thickened slightly. Stir in 1 cup pesto; cook just until heated through.

4. Pour sauce over pasta; stir gently to coat. Divide pasta among serving bowls; garnish with additional cheese.

THAI-STYLE BEEF
WITH PASTA ON LETTUCE

Makes 6 servings

3 tablespoons orange juice

2 tablespoons creamy peanut butter

2 tablespoons reduced-sodium soy sauce

1 tablespoon natural rice vinegar

2 teaspoons grated fresh ginger

6 ounces uncooked whole wheat spaghetti, broken in half

½ pound very lean (96% lean) ground beef

2 teaspoons minced garlic

2 cups (about 4 ounces) thinly sliced bok choy

½ cup (about 2 ounces) coarsely chopped carrot

4 green onions, cut into 1-inch pieces

¼ teaspoon red pepper flakes

6 pieces leaf lettuce

2 tablespoons (½ ounce) lightly salted dry roasted peanuts

1. Process orange juice, peanut butter, soy sauce, vinegar and ginger in food processor until nearly smooth. Set aside.

2. Cook spaghetti according to package directions. Drain and set aside.

3. Meanwhile, brown beef and garlic 6 to 8 minutes in large nonstick skillet over medium-high heat, stirring to break up meat; drain fat. Stir in bok choy, carrot, green onions and red pepper flakes. Drizzle with orange juice mixture. Reduce heat to medium; cover and cook 2 minutes.

4. Add hot spaghetti; toss until combined. Place lettuce leaves on serving plates. Spoon noodle mixture onto leaves and sprinkle with peanuts.

NEAPOLITAN PIZZA

Makes 4 servings

½ to ¾ cup warm water (105° to 115°F), divided

1 package (¼ ounce) active dry yeast

1 teaspoon sugar

2 cups all-purpose flour

1 tablespoon olive oil

½ teaspoon salt

1 cup Pizza Sauce (recipe follows)

2 cups (8 ounces) shredded mozzarella cheese

4 ounces sliced pepperoni (about 1 cup)

1 small green bell pepper, seeded and sliced

1 small onion, peeled and sliced

1 ounce grated Parmesan cheese (about ⅓ cup)

1. Combine ¼ cup water, yeast and sugar in small bowl. Stir to dissolve yeast; let stand about 5 minutes or until bubbly.

2. Measure flour, oil and salt into food processor; process 5 seconds. Add yeast mixture; process 10 seconds or until blended.

3. Turn on processor and very slowly drizzle just enough remaining water through feed tube so dough forms a ball that cleans side of bowl. Process until ball turns around bowl about 25 times. Let dough stand 1 to 2 minutes.

4. Turn on processor and gradually drizzle in enough remaining water to make dough soft, smooth and satiny but not sticky. Process until dough turns around bowl about 15 times.

5. Turn dough onto greased 14-inch pizza pan or large baking sheet. Shape dough into a ball. Cover with inverted bowl or plastic wrap and let stand 10 minutes.

6. Meanwhile, prepare Pizza Sauce. Preheat oven to 425°F.

7. Roll out or pat dough to cover pan, making slight ridge around edge. Spread Pizza Sauce evenly over dough; top with mozzarella cheese, pepperoni, bell pepper, onion and Parmesan cheese. Bake 15 to 20 minutes or until crust is golden.

PIZZA SAUCE

3   tomatoes, peeled, seeded and quartered

1   can (8 ounces) tomato sauce

½   teaspoon salt

1   to 2 teaspoons Italian seasoning or dried oregano

¼   teaspoon sugar

⅛   teaspoon black pepper

Process tomatoes in food processor using on/off pulse 3 or 4 times to coarsely chop. Add remaining ingredients; process until mixed.

ITALIAN BRIACOLE

Makes 6 servings

2 pounds boneless beef round steak, thinly sliced

2 slices whole grain bread, toasted and crumbled

½ cup chopped onion

¼ cup grated Parmesan cheese

2 cloves garlic

1 teaspoon Italian seasoning

1 egg

3 tablespoons olive oil, divided

½ teaspoon salt

½ teaspoon black pepper

1 jar (24 ounces) tomato basil pasta sauce

Hot cooked pasta (optional)

Chopped fresh Italian parsley (optional)

SLOW COOKER DIRECTIONS

1. Coat inside of slow cooker with nonstick cooking spray. Place round steak on large cutting board. Pound into ¼-inch thickness; cut evenly into two pieces.

2. Combine bread, onion, cheese, garlic, Italian seasoning, egg, 2 tablespoons oil, salt and pepper in food processor; pulse just until mixture is moistened but still chunky. Divide bread mixture evenly over steak pieces; roll tightly to enclose filling. Tie with kitchen string to secure.

3. Heat remaining 1 tablespoon oil in large skillet over medium heat. Add steak rolls; cook and turn 6 minutes or until browned on all sides. Pour ½ cup pasta sauce into bottom of slow cooker; top with steak rolls. Top with remaining pasta sauce. Cover; cook on LOW 4 to 5 hours. Remove steak pieces to large cutting board; cut each piece evenly into seven pieces. Serve over pasta, if desired. Garnish with parsley.

ON THE SIDE

WEDGE SALAD

Makes 4 servings

DRESSING

- ¾ cup mayonnaise
- ½ cup buttermilk
- 1 cup crumbled blue cheese, divided
- 1 clove garlic, minced
- ½ teaspoon sugar
- ⅛ teaspoon onion powder
- ⅛ teaspoon salt
- ⅛ teaspoon ground black pepper

SALAD

- 1 head iceberg lettuce
- 1 large tomato, diced (about 1 cup)
- ½ small red onion, cut into thin rings
- ½ cup crumbled crisp-cooked bacon (6 to 8 slices)

1. For dressing, combine mayonnaise, buttermilk, ½ cup cheese, garlic, sugar, onion powder, salt and pepper in food processor; process until smooth.

2. For salad, cut lettuce into quarters through stem end; remove stem from each wedge. Place wedges on individual serving plates; top with dressing. Sprinkle with tomato, onion, remaining ½ cup cheese and bacon.

POTATO AND LEEK GRATIN

Makes 6 to 8 servings

5   tablespoons butter, divided

2   large leeks, sliced

2   tablespoons minced garlic

2   pounds baking potatoes, peeled (about 4 medium)

1   cup whipping cream

1   cup milk

3   eggs

2   teaspoons salt

¼   teaspoon white pepper

2   to 3 slices dense day-old white bread, such as French or Italian

2   ounces grated Parmesan cheese

1. Preheat oven to 375°F. Generously grease shallow 2½-quart baking dish with 1 tablespoon butter.

2. Melt 2 tablespoons butter in large skillet over medium heat. Add leeks and garlic; cook and stir 8 to 10 minutes or until leeks are softened. Remove from heat.

3. Cut potatoes crosswise into ¹⁄₁₆-inch-thick slices. Layer half of potato slices in prepared baking dish; top with half of leek mixture. Repeat layers. Whisk cream, milk, eggs, salt and pepper in medium bowl until well blended; pour evenly over leek mixture.

4. Tear bread slices into 1-inch pieces. Place in food processor; process until fine crumbs form. Measure ¾ cup crumbs; place in small bowl. Stir in Parmesan cheese. Melt remaining 2 tablespoons butter; stir into crumb mixture. Sprinkle over vegetables in baking dish.

5. Bake 1 hour 15 minutes or until top is golden brown and potatoes are tender. Let stand 5 to 10 minutes before serving.

TANGY TAILGATE COLE SLAW

Makes 8 servings

1 small head cabbage (1½ to 2 pounds)

½ cup shredded carrots

½ cup mayonnaise

½ cup sour cream

¼ to ⅓ cup creamy horseradish sauce *or* 2 to 3 tablespoons prepared horseradish

2 to 3 tablespoons granulated sugar

¾ teaspoon salt

½ teaspoon celery salt

¼ teaspoon dry mustard

1. Core cabbage; cut into large chunks. Process in batches in food processor until cabbage is finely chopped. Transfer to large transportable bowl with cover. (Do not wash food processor.)

2. Stir carrots into cabbage. Add remaining ingredients to food processor; process until well combined; adjust horseradish and sugar to taste. Pour over cabbage; toss well. Cover; chill at least 8 hours or up to 24 hours.

CAULIFLOWER MASH

Makes 6 servings

2 heads cauliflower (to equal
   8 cups florets)

1 tablespoon butter

1 tablespoon half-and-half,
   milk or buttermilk

   Salt

SLOW COOKER DIRECTIONS

1. Break cauliflower into equal-size florets.
   Arrange cauliflower in slow cooker and add
   enough water to fill slow cooker (about
   2 inches). Cover; cook on LOW 5 to 6 hours.
   Drain well.

2. Place cooked cauliflower in food processor
   or blender; process until almost smooth.
   Add butter; process until smooth, adding
   half-and-half as needed to reach desired
   consistency. Season with salt.

SPINACH ARTICHOKE GRATIN

Makes 6 servings

2 cups (16 ounces) fat-free cottage cheese

½ cup cholesterol-free egg substitute

4½ tablespoons grated Parmesan cheese, divided

1 tablespoon lemon juice

⅛ teaspoon black pepper

⅛ teaspoon ground nutmeg

2 packages (10 ounces each) frozen chopped spinach, thawed

⅓ cup thinly sliced green onions

1 package (10 ounces) frozen artichoke hearts, thawed and halved

SLOW COOKER DIRECTIONS

1. Process cottage cheese, egg substitute, 3 tablespoons Parmesan cheese, lemon juice, pepper and nutmeg in food processor until smooth.

2. Spray slow cooker with nonstick cooking spray. Squeeze moisture from spinach. Combine spinach, cottage cheese mixture and green onions in large bowl. Spread half of mixture in slow cooker.

3. Pat artichoke halves dry with paper towels. Place in single layer over spinach mixture. Sprinkle with remaining Parmesan cheese. Cover with remaining spinach mixture. Cook, covered, with lid slightly ajar to allow excess moisture to escape, on LOW 3 to 3½ hours or on HIGH 2 to 2½ hours.

SWISS RÖSTI POTATOES

Makes 4 servings

4 large russet potatoes
   (about 6 ounces each)*

4 tablespoons butter or
   margarine

Salt and black pepper

Cherry tomato wedges and
   sprigs fresh rosemary
   (optional)

*Prepare potatoes several hours
or up to 1 day in advance.*

1. Preheat oven to 400°F. To prepare potatoes, scrub with soft vegetable brush under running water; rinse well. Pierce each potato in several places with fork. Bake 1 hour or until fork-tender. Cool completely, then refrigerate.

2. When potatoes are cold, peel with paring knife. Grate potatoes in food processor.

3. Heat butter in 10-inch skillet over medium-high heat until melted and bubbly. Press grated potatoes evenly into skillet. (Do not stir or turn potatoes.) Season with salt and pepper. Cook 10 to 12 minutes until golden brown.

4. Turn off heat; invert serving plate over skillet. Turn potatoes out onto plate. Garnish with tomatoes and rosemary, if desired. Serve immediately.

STRAWBERRY FIELDS SALAD

Makes 4 servings

GLAZED WALNUTS

- 2 tablespoons butter
- 6 tablespoons sugar
- 1 tablespoon honey
- ½ teaspoon salt
- ⅛ teaspoon ground red pepper
- 1 cup walnuts

DRESSING

- 1 cup fresh strawberries, hulled
- ½ cup vegetable oil
- 6 tablespoons white wine vinegar
- 3 tablespoons sugar
- 3 tablespoons honey
- 2 tablespoons balsamic vinegar
- 2 teaspoons Dijon mustard
- ½ teaspoon dried oregano
- ¼ teaspoon salt

SALAD

- 4 cups chopped romaine lettuce
- 4 cups coarsely chopped fresh spinach
- 1 cup sliced fresh strawberries
- ½ cup crumbled feta cheese
- 2 cups warm cooked chicken slices (about half of a rotisserie chicken)

1. For walnuts, preheat oven to 350°F. Line baking sheet with foil; spray with nonstick cooking spray.

2. Melt butter in medium skillet over medium-high heat. Stir in 6 tablespoons sugar, 1 tablespoon honey, ½ teaspoon salt and red pepper until well blended. Add walnuts; cook 3 minutes or until nuts are glazed and beginning to brown, stirring occasionally. Spread in single layer on prepared baking sheet. Bake 7 minutes or until nuts are lightly browned and fragrant. Cool completely on baking sheet. Break into individual nuts.

3. For dressing, combine strawberries, oil, vinegar, 3 tablespoons sugar, 3 tablespoons honey, balsamic vinegar, mustard, oregano and salt in food processor; blend 30 seconds or until smooth.

4. For salad, combine lettuce and spinach in large bowl. Top with sliced strawberries, glazed walnuts and feta. Toss with dressing; top with chicken.

CAULIFLOWER TABBOULEH

Makes 6 servings

2 packages (12 ounces each) cauliflower florets

3 tablespoons olive oil, divided

1 teaspoon curry powder

1 small bunch of flat leaf parsley

1 medium onion, finely chopped (¾ cup)

½ seedless cucumber, chopped (1½ cups)

1 cup chopped ripe tomato *or* 1 can (about 14 ounces) no-salt-added diced tomatoes, well drained

⅓ cup fresh lemon juice

½ teaspoon black pepper

¼ teaspoon salt

Romaine lettuce

1. Cut large cauliflower florets into uniform pieces. Place cauliflower in food processor; pulse 1 minute or until chopped into uniform granules.

2. Heat 1 tablespoon oil in large nonstick skillet over medium-high heat. Add curry powder; cook until sizzling. Add cauliflower; stir-fry about 10 minutes or until cooked through. Remove from heat and cool.

3. Meanwhile, rinse parsley, trim and discard large stems. Place parsley sprigs in food processor; pulse 10 to 20 seconds to chop.

4. Combine cauliflower mixture, parsley, onion, cucumber and tomato in large bowl. Whisk remaining 2 tablespoons oil, lemon juice, pepper and salt in small bowl. Pour over cauliflower mixture; toss well. Serve at room temperature or chilled on romaine lettuce leaves.

POTATO PANCAKES
WITH APPLE-CHERRY CHUTNEY

Makes 6 servings

Apple-Cherry Chutney
(recipe follows)

1 pound baking potatoes
(about 2 medium)

½ small onion

3 egg whites

2 tablespoons all-purpose
flour

½ teaspoon salt

¼ teaspoon black pepper

4 teaspoons vegetable oil,
divided

Fresh mint

1. Prepare Apple-Cherry Chutney; set aside.

2. Wash and scrub potatoes; cut into chunks. Combine potatoes, onion, egg whites, flour, salt and pepper in food processor; process until almost smooth (mixture will appear grainy).

3. Heat large nonstick skillet 1 minute over medium heat. Add 1 teaspoon oil. Spoon ⅓ cup batter per pancake into skillet. Cook 3 pancakes at a time, 3 minutes per side or until golden brown. Repeat with remaining batter, adding 1 teaspoon oil with each batch. Serve with Apple-Cherry Chutney. Garnish with mint.

APPLE-CHERRY CHUTNEY

Makes 1½ cups

1 cup chunky applesauce

½ cup canned tart cherries,
drained

2 tablespoons packed brown
sugar

1 teaspoon lemon juice

½ teaspoon ground cinnamon

⅛ teaspoon ground nutmeg

Combine all ingredients in small saucepan; bring to a boil. Reduce heat; simmer 5 minutes. Serve warm.

SMOOTHIES & REFRESHERS

MANDARIN ORANGE, COCONUT AND LIME COOLER

Makes 2 servings

1 can (15 ounces) mandarin oranges in light syrup, undrained

2 tablespoons corn syrup

1 tablespoon lime juice

1 teaspoon grated lime peel

1 teaspoon grated fresh ginger

1 teaspoon coconut extract

½ teaspoon orange extract

1 cup ice cubes

Sprigs fresh basil or mint (optional)

Lime slices (optional)

1. Combine oranges with juice, corn syrup, lime juice, lime peel, ginger, coconut extract, orange extract and ice cubes in food processor; process 10 seconds or until ice is crushed.

2. Pour into two glasses. Garnish with basil sprigs and lime slices. Serve immediately.

SPICED PASSION FRUIT-YOGURT SMOOTHIE

Makes 3 servings

1 cup vanilla nonfat Greek yogurt

1 cup sliced fresh strawberries

1 ripe banana, cut into pieces

¼ cup frozen passion fruit juice concentrate, thawed

¾ teaspoon pumpkin pie spice

⅛ teaspoon ground white pepper

1. Combine yogurt, strawberries, banana, juice concentrate, pumpkin pie spice and white pepper in food processor; process until smooth.

2. Pour into three glasses. Serve immediately.

CHOCOLATE-BLUEBERRY SOY SHAKE

Makes 1 serving

½ cup plus 2 tablespoons
   soymilk

¼ cup crushed ice

2 tablespoons fresh or
   frozen blueberries
   (about 20 berries)

¼ teaspoon unsweetened
   cocoa powder

1. Combine soymilk, ice, blueberries and cocoa in food processor; process until smooth.

2. Pour into chilled glass. Serve immediately.

FROSTY RASPBERRY LEMON TEA

Makes 2 servings

1½ cups ice

1 cup brewed lemon-flavored herbal tea, at room temperature

1 cup water

½ cup frozen unsweetened raspberries

1. Combine all ingredients in food processor; process until smooth, pulsing to break up ice.

2. Pour into two glasses. Serve immediately.

ICED COFFEE FRAPPÉ

Makes 2 servings

1 cup strong brewed coffee, cooled

½ cup reduced-fat (2%) milk

2 tablespoons sugar

1 tablespoon light chocolate syrup

Ice cubes

1. Combine coffee, milk, sugar, chocolate syrup and ice in food processor; process until smooth.

2. Pour into two glasses. Serve immediately.

VARIATIONS: Substitute ½ teaspoon vanilla, almond extract or ½ teaspoon ground cinnamon for chocolate syrup.

ROOTY TOOTY GRAPEFRUITY

Makes 2 servings

3 tablespoons sugar, divided

1 to 2 drops red food
coloring (optional)

1 fresh ruby red grapefruit,
peeled and seeded with
membrane removed

1 cup crushed ice

¼ to ½ cup grapefruit juice

Sprigs fresh lavender or
rosemary (optional)

1. Tint 1 tablespoon sugar with food coloring,
if desired. Moisten rims of two glasses; dip
in sugar.

2. Combine grapefruit, ice, grapefruit juice
and remaining 2 tablespoons sugar in food
processor; process until smooth.

3. Pour into prepared glasses. Garnish each
serving with lavender sprigs.

TIP: To tint the sugar, place it in a resealable
food storage bag. Add the food coloring, seal
the bag and shake until sugar is evenly tinted.

PEACHY RAZZ REFRESHER

Makes 2 servings

1 cup ice

1 cup frozen sliced peaches

½ cup frozen raspberries

½ cup plain nonfat yogurt

½ cup orange juice

Fresh peach slices
(optional)

Fresh raspberries
(optional)

1. Combine ice, peaches, frozen raspberries, yogurt and orange juice in food processor; process until smooth.

2. Pour into two glasses. Garnish with peach slices and fresh raspberries. Serve immediately.

BEET & BERRY BLAST

Makes 2 servings

½ cup canned sliced beets

½ cup frozen mixed berries

½ cup no-sugar-added
  orange juice

1 tablespoon lemon juice

1 tablespoon honey

  Ice

Combine all ingredients in food processor;
process until smooth. Pour into serving glasses.

ICED CAPPUCCINO

Makes 2 servings

1 cup fat-free vanilla frozen yogurt or fat-free vanilla ice cream

1 cup cold strong brewed coffee

1 packet sugar substitute *or* equivalent of 2 teaspoons sugar

1 teaspoon unsweetened cocoa powder

1 teaspoon vanilla

1. Combine all ingredients in food processor; process until smooth. Place container in freezer; freeze 1½ to 2 hours or until top and sides of mixture are partially frozen.

2. Scrape sides of container; process until smooth and frothy.

3. Pour into two glasses. Garnish as desired. Serve immediately.

ICED MOCHA CAPPUCCINO: Increase amount of cocoa to 1 tablespoon. Proceed as directed above.

TIP: To add an extra flavor boost to this refreshing drink, add orange peel, lemon peel or a dash of ground cinnamon to your coffee grounds before brewing.

RASPBERRY LEMONADE SLUSHIES

Makes 6 servings

1½ cups fresh or frozen
   raspberries

½ can (12 ounces) frozen
   lemonade concentrate

1 cup water

4 cups ice cubes

1. Combine raspberries, lemonade concentrate and water in food processor; process until smooth. Add ice; process until desired consistency is reached.

2. Pour into six glasses. Serve immediately.

SWEET ENDINGS

CHOCOLATE FUDGE CHEESECAKE PARFAITS

Makes 4 servings

1½ cups fat-free cottage cheese

4 packets sugar substitute *or* equivalent of 8 teaspoons sugar

2 teaspoons packed brown sugar

1½ teaspoons vanilla

2 tablespoons semisweet mini chocolate chips, divided

2 cups fat-free chocolate ice cream or fat-free frozen yogurt

3 tablespoons graham cracker crumbs

1. Combine cottage cheese, sugar substitute, brown sugar and vanilla in food processor; process until smooth. Stir in 1 tablespoon mini chips with wooden spoon.

2. Spoon about ¼ cup ice cream into each stemmed glass. Top with heaping tablespoon cheese mixture; sprinkle with 2 teaspoons graham cracker crumbs. Repeat layers. Freeze parfaits 15 to 30 minutes to firm slightly.

3. Garnish each parfait with remaining 1 tablespoon mini chips and remaining cracker crumbs.

COOKIES & CREAM POPS

Makes 3 pops

1 cup crushed mini creme-filled cookies (about 2½ cups cookies), divided

⅓ cup plus 1 tablespoon milk, divided

3 (5-ounce) plastic or paper cups or pop molds

1¼ cups vanilla ice cream

¼ cup mini semisweet chocolate chips

⅛ teaspoon ground cinnamon

3 pop sticks

1. Combine ½ cup cookie crumbs and 1 tablespoon milk in small bowl, mixing and mashing with fork until blended. Press about 2 tablespoons crumb mixture into each mold, using wet fingers if necessary.

2. Combine remaining ½ cup cookie crumbs, ⅓ cup milk, ice cream, chocolate chips and cinnamon in food processor; process until smooth.

3. Layer mixture into cups over cookie base. Cover top of each cup with small piece of foil. Insert sticks through center of foil. Freeze 6 hours or until firm.

4. To remove pops from molds, remove foil and place bottoms of pops under warm running water until loosened. Press firmly on bottoms to release. (Do not twist or pull sticks.)

SWEET POTATO COCONUT BARS

Makes 16 bars

30 shortbread cookies, crushed

1¼ cups finely chopped walnuts, toasted,* divided

¾ cup sweetened flaked coconut, divided

¼ cup (½ stick) butter, softened

2 cans (16 ounces each) sweet potatoes, well drained and mashed (2 cups)

2 eggs

1 teaspoon ground cinnamon

½ teaspoon ground ginger

¼ to ½ teaspoon ground cloves

¼ teaspoon salt

1 can (14 ounces) sweetened condensed milk

¾ cup butterscotch chips

To toast walnuts, spread in single layer on baking sheet. Bake in preheated 350°F oven 8 to 10 minutes or until golden brown, stirring frequently.

1. Preheat oven to 350°F.

2. Combine cookie crumbs, 1 cup chopped walnuts, ½ cup coconut and butter in food processor; process using on/off pulses until well combined. Press two thirds of mixture onto bottom of 8-inch square baking pan.

3. Beat sweet potatoes, eggs, cinnamon, ginger, cloves and salt in large bowl with electric mixer at medium-low speed until well blended. Gradually add sweetened condensed milk; beat until well blended. Spoon filling evenly over prepared crust. Top with remaining crumb mixture, pressing lightly.

4. Bake 45 to 50 minutes or until knife inserted into center comes out clean. Sprinkle evenly with butterscotch chips, remaining ¼ cup walnuts and ¼ cup coconut. Bake 5 minutes. Cool completely in pan on wire rack. Cover and refrigerate 2 hours before serving.

ST. PATTY'S POPS

Makes 3 pops

½ cup crushed chocolate-covered mint cookies

⅓ cup plus 1 tablespoon milk, divided

3 (5-ounce) plastic or paper cups or pop molds

1¼ cups mint chocolate chip ice cream

3 pop sticks

6 tablespoons quick-hardening chocolate shell dessert topping

1. Combine cookie crumbs and 1 tablespoon milk in small bowl, mixing and mashing with fork until well blended. Press about 2 tablespoons crumb mixture into each cup, using wet fingers if necessary.

2. Combine remaining ⅓ cup milk and ice cream in food processor; process until smooth.

3. Layer mixture into cups over cookie base. Freeze 1 hour.

4. Insert sticks. Spoon 2 tablespoons chocolate shell topping into each cup over ice cream mixture. *Do not cover with foil.* Freeze 4 hours or until firm.

5. To serve, gently twist frozen pops out of plastic cups or peel away paper cups.

TIP: Make these plain pops more appealing by using plastic cups, which give the pops a ridged texture.

MANGO-ORANGE MOUSSE

Makes 6 to 8 servings

1 large can (28 ounces)
   mangoes *or* 2 small
   cans (15 ounces each)
   mangoes, drained

1 envelope (¼ ounce)
   unflavored gelatin

¼ cup cold water

3 eggs,* at room
   temperature, separated

¾ cup orange juice

½ cup sugar, divided

1 tablespoon lemon juice

   Dash salt

2 tablespoons rum

1 cup whipping cream,
   divided

   Shredded orange peel
   (optional)

   Sprig fresh mint (optional)

*Use only grade A clean,
uncracked eggs.*

1. Process enough of the mangoes in food processor to make 1 cup purée. Thinly slice remaining mangoes; cover. Refrigerate; reserve for garnish.

2. Sprinkle gelatin over cold water in small bowl; let stand 1 minute to soften. Beat egg yolks with whisk in medium heavy saucepan. Whisk in orange juice, ¼ cup sugar, lemon juice and salt. Cook over medium-low heat, stirring constantly, until mixture has thickened enough to lightly coat metal spoon. Remove from heat.

3. Add softened gelatin to saucepan; stir until dissolved. Stir in mango purée and rum. Refrigerate until mixture mounds slightly when dropped from spoon.

4. Beat egg whites in large bowl with electric mixer at high speed until frothy. Gradually add remaining ¼ cup sugar, 1 tablespoon at a time, beating well after each addition. Beat until stiff peaks form; fold into mango mixture. Without washing bowl or beaters, beat ½ cup cream until soft peaks form. Fold into mango mixture. Spoon into glass serving bowl. Refrigerate until firm, 3 to 4 hours or up to 24 hours.

5. Just before serving, beat remaining ½ cup cream until soft peaks form. Garnish mousse with reserved mango slices, whipped cream, orange peel and mint.

BAKLAVA

Makes about 32 pieces

4 cups walnuts, shelled pistachio nuts and/or slivered almonds (1 pound)

1¼ cups sugar, divided

2 teaspoons ground cinnamon

¼ teaspoon ground cloves

1 cup (2 sticks) butter, melted

1 package (16 ounces) frozen phyllo dough (about 20 sheets), thawed

1½ cups water

¾ cup honey

2 (2-inch-long) strips lemon peel

1 tablespoon fresh lemon juice

1 cinnamon stick

3 whole cloves

1. Place half of walnuts in food processor. Process using on/off pulses until nuts are finely chopped, but not pasty. Transfer to large bowl; repeat with remaining nuts. Add ½ cup sugar, ground cinnamon and ground cloves to nuts; mix well.

2. Preheat oven to 325°F. Brush 13×9-inch baking dish with some of melted butter or line with foil, leaving overhang on two sides for easy removal. Unroll phyllo dough and place on large sheet of waxed paper. Trim phyllo sheets to 13×9 inches. Cover phyllo with plastic wrap and damp, clean kitchen towel. (Phyllo dough dries out quickly if not covered.)

3. Place 1 phyllo sheet in bottom of dish, folding in edges if too long; brush surface with butter. Repeat with 7 more phyllo sheets, brushing surface of each sheet with butter as they are layered. Sprinkle about ½ cup nut mixture evenly over layered phyllo. Top nuts with 3 more layers of phyllo, brushing each sheet with butter. Sprinkle another ½ cup nut mixture on top. Repeat layering and brushing of 3 phyllo sheets with ½ cup nut mixture until there are a total of eight layers. Top final layer of nut mixture with remaining phyllo sheets, brushing each sheet with butter.

4. Score baklava lengthwise into 4 equal sections, then cut diagonally at 1½-inch intervals to form diamond shapes. Sprinkle top lightly with some water to prevent top phyllo layers from curling up during baking. Bake 50 to 60 minutes or until golden brown.

5. For syrup, combine 1½ cups water, remaining ¾ cup sugar, honey, lemon peel, lemon juice, cinnamon stick and whole cloves in medium saucepan. Bring to a boil over high heat. Reduce heat to low; simmer 15 minutes. Strain hot syrup; drizzle evenly over hot baklava. Cool completely. Cut baklava into pieces along score lines.

FRESH STRAWBERRY-CREAM CHEESE TART

Makes 8 servings

Pastry for single-crust
9-inch pie

8 ounces reduced-fat cream
cheese, softened

¼ cup *plus* 1 tablespoon
thawed frozen
unsweetened pineapple
juice concentrate, divided

1½ pints fresh strawberries,*
hulled and halved (about
4 cups strawberry halves)

½ cup no-sugar-added
strawberry fruit spread

Do not use frozen strawberries.

1. Preheat oven to 350°F. Roll out pastry to 12-inch circle; place in 10-inch tart pan with removable bottom or 10-inch quiche dish. Trim edge of pastry ¼ inch above edge of tart pan to allow for shrinkage or flute decoratively in quiche dish. Prick bottom and sides of pastry with fork. Bake 12 to 15 minutes or until golden brown. Cool completely on wire rack.

2. Process cream cheese with food processor until creamy. Gradually add ¼ cup pineapple juice concentrate, pulsing until smooth. Spread evenly over cooled pastry; top with strawberries. Combine fruit spread and remaining 1 tablespoon pineapple juice concentrate; mix well. Brush evenly over strawberries. Serve immediately or cover and refrigerate up to 2 hours before serving.

WATERMELON ICE

Makes 6 servings

4 cups seeded 1-inch watermelon chunks

¼ cup thawed frozen unsweetened pineapple juice concentrate

2 tablespoons fresh lime juice

Fresh melon balls (optional)

Fresh mint leaves (optional)

1. Place melon chunks in single layer in large resealable freezer food storage bag; freeze 8 hours or until firm.

2. Place frozen melon in food processor. Let stand 15 to 20 minutes to soften slightly. Add pineapple juice concentrate and lime juice. Remove feed tube plunger from top of food processor to allow air to be incorporated. Process until smooth, scraping down sides of container frequently.

3. Spoon into individual dessert dishes. Garnish with melon balls and mint leaves, if desired. Serve immediately.

HONEYDEW ICE: Substitute honeydew for watermelon and unsweetened pineapple-guava-orange juice concentrate for pineapple juice concentrate.

CANTALOUPE ICE: Substitute cantaloupe for watermelon and unsweetened pineapple-guava-orange juice concentrate for pineapple juice concentrate.

NOTE: Ices can be transferred to airtight container and frozen up to 1 month. Let stand at room temperature 10 minutes to soften slightly before serving.

RASPBERRY MOUSSE

Makes 4 cups

1 package (10 ounces) frozen raspberries in syrup

1 package (4-serving size) raspberry-flavored gelatin

¼ cup water

2 cups whipping cream

1. Process raspberries with syrup in food processor until smooth. Press through fine-mesh sieve to remove seeds. Set aside.

2. Heat gelatin and water in small saucepan over medium heat 5 to 7 minutes or until mixture is very syrupy, stirring occasionally. Remove from heat. Cool slightly.

3. Beat cream in large bowl with electric mixer at high speed 3 to 5 minutes or until soft peaks form. Add raspberries and gelatin mixture; beat 3 to 5 minutes or until well blended.

4. Pour into individual serving dishes; refrigerate 2 hours or until set.

BANANA & CHOCOLATE CHIP POPS

Makes 4 servings

1 small ripe banana

1 container (8 ounces) banana nonfat yogurt

1/8 teaspoon ground nutmeg

2 tablespoons mini semisweet chocolate chips

4 (5-ounce) plastic or paper cups or pop molds

4 pop sticks

1. Slice banana; place in food processor. Add yogurt and nutmeg; process until smooth. Transfer to small bowl; stir in chips.

2. Spoon banana mixture into cups. Cover top of each cup with small piece of foil. Insert sticks through center of foil. Set on level surface in freezer; freeze 2 hours or until firm. To unmold, briefly run warm water over cups until each pop loosens.

FRUIT TART

Makes 8 to 10 servings

CRUST

2 whole wheat naan
(6 ounces total), torn into
large pieces

3 tablespoons sugar

4 tablespoons melted butter

FILLING

8 ounces cream cheese,
cut into 1-inch cubes,
softened

3 tablespoons sugar

1 tablespoon lemon juice

1 teaspoon vanilla

TOPPING

2 kiwi, peeled and sliced

Assorted fresh berries

2 tablespoons apricot jam,
warmed

1. Preheat oven to 350°F. Line baking sheet with parchment paper; place 9-inch round fluted tart pan on top.

2. Place naan pieces in food processor. Process until fine crumbs form, yielding about 2 cups. Add sugar, pulse to incorporate. Add butter, pulse until combined, about 15 pulses.

3. Press crumbs firmly in bottom and up sides of tart pan. Bake 25 to 30 minutes until crust is set and golden brown. Place on wire rack; cool completely.

4. Beat cream cheese, sugar, lemon juice and vanilla on medium speed of electric mixer. Pour filling into cooled tart shell, smoothing evenly with spatula.

5. Arrange kiwi and berries on top of tart. Brush fruit with warmed jam. Refrigerate 20 minutes before serving.

WARM APPLE CROSTATA

Makes 4 tarts

1¾ cups all-purpose flour

⅓ cup granulated sugar

½ teaspoon plus ⅛ teaspoon salt, divided

¾ cup (1½ sticks) cold butter, cut into small pieces

3 tablespoons ice water

2 teaspoons vanilla

8 Pink Lady or Honeycrisp apples (about 1½ pounds), peeled and cut into ¼-inch slices

¼ cup packed brown sugar

1 tablespoon lemon juice

1 teaspoon ground cinnamon

⅛ teaspoon ground nutmeg

4 teaspoons butter, cut into very small pieces

1 egg, beaten

1 to 2 teaspoons coarse sugar

Vanilla ice cream

Caramel sauce or ice cream topping

1. Combine flour, ⅓ cup granulated sugar and ½ teaspoon salt in food processor; process 5 seconds. Add ¾ cup butter; process about 10 seconds or until mixture resembles coarse crumbs.

2. Combine ice water and vanilla in small bowl. With motor running, pour mixture through feed tube; process 12 seconds or until dough begins to come together. Shape dough into a disc; wrap in plastic wrap and refrigerate 30 minutes.

3. Meanwhile, combine apples, brown sugar, lemon juice, cinnamon, nutmeg and remaining ⅛ teaspoon salt in large bowl; toss to coat. Preheat oven to 400°F.

4. Line two baking sheets with parchment paper. Cut dough into four pieces; roll out each piece into 7-inch circle on floured surface. Place circles on prepared baking sheets; mound apples in center of dough circles (about 1 cup apples for each crostata). Fold or roll up edges of dough towards center to create rim of crostata. Dot apples with remaining 4 teaspoons butter. Brush dough with egg; sprinkle dough and apples with coarse sugar.

5. Bake about 20 minutes or until apples are tender and crust is golden brown. Serve warm topped with ice cream and caramel sauce.

CINNAMON PLUM WALNUT COBBLER

Makes 9 servings

¾ cup all-purpose flour

½ cup chopped walnuts

½ cup plus 3 tablespoons granulated sugar, divided

⅛ teaspoon salt

6 tablespoons (¾ stick) cold butter, cut into small pieces

1 to 2 tablespoons milk, plus additional for brushing top of dough

8 red plums (about 2½ pounds), cut into ¼-inch slices

2½ tablespoons cornstarch

¾ teaspoon ground cinnamon, divided

Mascarpone Cream (recipe follows)

1. Preheat oven to 350°F. Spray 8-inch square baking dish with nonstick cooking spray.

2. Combine flour, walnuts, 1 tablespoon granulated sugar and salt in food processor. Add butter; process until butter is incorporated into mixture. With motor running, add just enough milk through feed tube to form soft dough. Wrap with plastic wrap; refrigerate 30 minutes.

3. Combine plums, ½ cup granulated sugar, cornstarch and ½ teaspoon cinnamon in large bowl; toss to coat. Spread fruit mixture evenly in prepared baking dish.

4. Bake 30 minutes. Meanwhile, roll out dough into 8-inch square. Cut out nine circles with 2¼-inch round cookie cutter. Remove scraps of dough; crumble over baked fruit or discard. Arrange dough circles over fruit; brush lightly with additional milk. Combine remaining 2 tablespoons sugar and ¼ teaspoon cinnamon in small bowl; sprinkle over dough.

5. Bake 30 to 35 minutes or until topping is golden brown. Meanwhile, prepare Mascarpone Cream. Serve with warm cobbler.

MASCARPONE CREAM: Combine ½ cup mascarpone, 2 tablespoons powdered sugar and 2 tablespoons milk in small bowl; whisk until smooth.

PECAN-QUINOA CRUSTED PUMPKIN PIE

Makes 8 servings

CRUST

- 1 package (4 ounces) chopped pecans
- ⅓ cup uncooked quinoa, preferably the tri-colored variety
- ¼ cup packed dark brown sugar
- ¼ teaspoon salt
- 1 egg

FILLING

- 1 can (30 ounces) pumpkin pie mix
- 1 can (5 ounces) evaporated milk
- 2 eggs
- 1 cup whipped topping
- ⅛ teaspoon ground cinnamon (optional)

1. Preheat oven to 350°F. Spray 9-inch deep dish pie pan with nonstick cooking spray.

2. Place pecans, quinoa, brown sugar and ¼ teaspoon salt in food processor. Pulse about 2 minutes or until mixture is finely ground; scraping down sides occasionally. Add egg; pulse until blended. Place mixture in prepared pan. Using back of spoon or fork, gently smooth mixture over bottom and slightly up sides until evenly distributed. Bake 18 to 20 minutes or until slightly firm to touch and edges are slightly golden brown.

3. Meanwhile, combine pie mix, evaporated milk and 2 eggs in food processor; blend until smooth.

4. Pour pumpkin mixture into pie crust; place on baking sheet. Bake 1 hour 15 minutes or until knife inserted near center comes out clean. Cool to room temperature. Cover; refrigerate overnight.

5. When ready to serve, top with whipped topping and sprinkle with cinnamon, if desired.

TIPS: No need to clean the food processor before combining pumpkin mixture—saves steps and energy!

For peak flavor and texture, be sure to refrigerate overnight before serving. This allows flavors to blend and quinoa to soften slightly.

BERRY CHEESECAKE WITH QUINOA-GRAHAM CRUST

Makes 8 to 10 servings

CRUST

½ cup uncooked quinoa, preferably the white grain variety

8 full graham cracker sheets

¼ cup sugar

⅓ cup butter, softened

FILLING

⅔ cup sugar

3 packages (8 ounces each) cream cheese, softened

3 eggs

2 teaspoons vanilla

TOPPING

1 quart fresh strawberries, hulled and quartered

1 cup fresh or frozen raspberries

⅓ cup sugar

½ teaspoon vanilla

1. Preheat oven to 375°F. Coat 9-inch springform pan with nonstick cooking spray.

2. Combine quinoa, graham crackers and ¼ cup sugar in food processor. Secure lid; process about 2 minutes to fine texture. Add butter; pulse until blended.

3. Place mixture in prepared pan; press lightly on bottom. Bake 8 minutes or until slightly golden on edges; place on wire rack to cool slightly.

4. *Reduce oven temperature to 325°F.* Combine ⅔ cup sugar, cream cheese, eggs and 2 teaspoons vanilla in food processor; process until well blended. Pour filling over crust.

5. Place pan on baking sheet; bake on center oven rack 55 minutes or until center is almost set.

6. Meanwhile, combine berries, ⅓ cup sugar and ½ teaspoon vanilla in large bowl. Cover; chill in refrigerator until needed.

7. Remove cheesecake from oven. Cool on wire rack. Cover; refrigerate overnight.

8. To serve, top cheesecake slices with berry mixture.

S'MORES IN A JAR

Makes 8 (½-pint) jars

CRUST

1 sleeve honey graham crackers (9 whole crackers)

¼ cup (½ stick) butter, melted

¼ teaspoon salt

CHOCOLATE MOUSSE

1 cup semisweet chocolate chips

2 cups chilled whipping cream, divided

4 egg yolks

Pinch of salt

1 teaspoon vanilla

¼ cup sugar

MARSHMALLOW TOPPING

1 jar (7 ounces) marshmallow creme

1 cup mini marshmallows

1. For crust, place graham crackers in food processor; process until coarse crumbs form. Add butter and ¼ teaspoon salt; process until blended. Press 2 tablespoons mixture into each of eight wide-mouth ½-pint jars. Freeze 10 minutes.

2. Heat chocolate chips in medium saucepan over low heat until melted, stirring frequently. Remove from heat and stir in ¼ cup whipping cream.

3. Place egg yolks and pinch of salt in medium bowl. Whisk about half of chocolate mixture into egg yolks; whisk egg yolk mixture back into chocolate mixture in saucepan. Cook over low heat 2 minutes, whisking constantly. Remove from heat; cool 5 minutes.

4. Beat remaining 1¾ cups whipping cream and vanilla to soft peaks in medium bowl. Gradually beat in sugar; continue beating until stiff peaks form. Stir about one fourth of whipped cream into chocolate mixture; fold chocolate mixture into remaining whipped cream until completely combined.

5. Scoop heaping spoonful of marshmallow creme on top of crust in each jar. Press into even layer with dampened hands. Top with heaping ¼ cup mousse.

6. For garnish, preheat broiler. Spray small baking pan with nonstick cooking spray. Spread marshmallows in prepared pan. Broil about 30 seconds or until marshmallows are toasted. Scoop toasted marshmallows on top of each serving; sprinkle with additional graham cracker mixture, if desired.

KEY LIME MINIS

Makes 4 (½-pint) jars

6 whole graham crackers

2 tablespoons butter

Pinch of salt

1 tablespoon whipping
cream or milk

1 can (14 ounces) sweetened
condensed milk

6 tablespoons key lime juice

3 egg yolks

1 drop *each* yellow and
green food coloring

Whipped topping
(optional)

Lime slices (optional)

1. Place graham crackers in food processor;
pulse until coarse crumbs form. Add butter,
salt and cream; pulse until well blended.

2. Whisk sweetened condensed milk, lime juice,
egg yolks and food coloring in medium
saucepan. Cook over medium-low heat 5 to
7 minutes, whisking frequently. Remove from
heat; cool 10 minutes.

3. Press 2 heaping tablespoons crumb mixture
into bottom of four ½-pint jars. Top evenly
with lime mixture.

4. Refrigerate overnight. Top with whipped
topping and lime slices, as desired.

CHOCOLATE PEANUT BUTTER PIE

Makes 8 servings

10 whole chocolate graham crackers, broken into pieces

2 tablespoons granulated sugar

¼ cup (½ stick) butter, melted

1 package (8 ounces) cream cheese, softened

1 cup creamy peanut butter

1¾ cups powdered sugar, divided

3 tablespoons butter, softened

1¾ teaspoons vanilla, divided

¼ teaspoon salt

2 cups cold whipping cream

½ cup unsweetened cocoa powder

2 packages (1½ ounces each) chocolate peanut butter cups, chopped

Hot fudge sauce, heated (optional)

1. Preheat oven to 350°F. Combine graham crackers and granulated sugar in food processor; process until finely ground. Add ¼ cup melted butter; process until well blended. Press into bottom and up side of 9-inch pie plate.

2. Bake 8 minutes. Cool completely on wire rack.

3. Meanwhile, beat cream cheese, peanut butter, ¾ cup powdered sugar, 3 tablespoons butter, 1 teaspoon vanilla and salt in large bowl with electric mixer about 3 minutes or until light and fluffy. Spread filling in cooled crust; smooth top. Refrigerate pie while preparing topping.

4. Beat cream, cocoa, remaining 1 cup powdered sugar and ¾ teaspoon vanilla in medium bowl with electric mixer at high speed 1 to 2 minutes or until soft peaks form. Spread chocolate whipped cream over peanut butter layer; sprinkle with peanut butter cups. Refrigerate several hours or overnight.

5. Drizzle serving plates with hot fudge sauce, if desired. Serve pie over sauce.

KEY LIME PIE

Makes 8 servings

12 whole graham crackers*

⅓ cup butter, melted

3 tablespoons sugar

2 cans (14 ounces each) sweetened condensed milk

¾ cup key lime juice

6 egg yolks

Pinch of salt

Whipped cream (optional)

Lime slices (optional)

Or substitute 1½ cups graham cracker crumbs.

1. Preheat oven to 350°F. Spray 9-inch pie plate or springform pan with nonstick cooking spray.

2. Place graham crackers in food processor; pulse until coarse crumbs form. Add butter and sugar; pulse until well blended. Press mixture onto bottom and 1 inch up side of prepared pie plate. Bake 8 minutes or until lightly browned. Remove to wire rack to cool 10 minutes. *Reduce oven temperature to 325°F.*

3. Meanwhile, beat sweetened condensed milk, lime juice, egg yolks and salt in large bowl with electric mixer at medium-low speed 1 minute or until well blended and smooth. Pour into crust.

4. Bake 20 minutes or until top is set. Cool completely in pan on wire rack. Cover and refrigerate 2 hours or overnight. Garnish with whipped cream and lime slices.

TOFFEE CAKE WITH WHISKEY SAUCE

Makes 9 servings

8 ounces chopped dates

2¼ teaspoons baking soda, divided

1½ cups boiling water

2 cups all-purpose flour

½ teaspoon salt

¾ cup (1½ sticks) butter, softened

½ cup granulated sugar

½ cup packed dark brown sugar

2 eggs

1 teaspoon vanilla

1½ cups butterscotch sauce

2 tablespoons whiskey

1 cup glazed pecans* or chopped toasted pecans

Vanilla ice cream

*Glazed pecans can be found in the produce section of many supermarkets with other salad toppings.

1. Preheat oven to 350°F. Spray 9-inch square baking pan with nonstick cooking spray.

2. Combine dates and 1½ teaspoons baking soda in medium bowl. Stir in boiling water; let stand 10 minutes to soften. Process in food processor until mixture forms paste.

3. Combine flour, remaining ¾ teaspoon baking soda and salt in medium bowl; mix well. Beat butter, granulated sugar and brown sugar in large bowl with electric mixer at medium speed 3 minutes or until creamy. Add eggs, one at a time, beating until well blended. Beat in vanilla. Add flour mixture alternately with date mixture at low speed just until blended. Spread batter in prepared pan.

4. Bake 30 minutes or until toothpick inserted into center comes out with moist crumbs. Cool in pan on wire rack 15 minutes. Cut cake into nine squares; place on serving plates.

5. Heat butterscotch sauce in medium microwavable bowl on HIGH 30 seconds or until warm; stir in whiskey. Drizzle glaze over cake; sprinkle with pecans and top with ice cream.

ICE CREAM PIZZA TREAT

Makes 8 servings

24 chocolate sandwich
   cookies

1 jar (about 12 ounces) hot
   fudge topping, divided

2 pints vanilla ice cream

⅓ cup candy-coated
   chocolate pieces

1. Place cookies in food processor; pulse until large crumbs form. (Do not overprocess into fine crumbs.) Add ½ cup fudge topping; pulse just until blended. (Mixture should not be smooth; small cookie pieces may remain.)

2. Transfer mixture to pizza pan; press into even 11- to 12-inch layer about ¼ inch thick. Freeze crust 10 minutes. Meanwhile, remove ice cream from freezer to soften 10 minutes.

3. Spread ice cream evenly over crust (about ½-inch-thick layer), leaving ½-inch border. Return to freezer; freeze 2 hours or until firm.

4. Heat remaining fudge topping according to package directions. Drizzle over ice cream; top with chocolate pieces. Freeze 1 hour or until firm. Cut into wedges to serve.

INDEX

METRIC CONVERSION CHART

VOLUME MEASUREMENTS (dry)

1/8 teaspoon = 0.5 mL
1/4 teaspoon = 1 mL
1/2 teaspoon = 2 mL
3/4 teaspoon = 4 mL
1 teaspoon = 5 mL
1 tablespoon = 15 mL
2 tablespoons = 30 mL
1/4 cup = 60 mL
1/3 cup = 75 mL
1/2 cup = 125 mL
2/3 cup = 150 mL
3/4 cup = 175 mL
1 cup = 250 mL
2 cups = 1 pint = 500 mL
3 cups = 750 mL
4 cups = 1 quart = 1 L

VOLUME MEASUREMENTS (fluid)

1 fluid ounce (2 tablespoons) = 30 mL
4 fluid ounces (1/2 cup) = 125 mL
8 fluid ounces (1 cup) = 250 mL
12 fluid ounces (1 1/2 cups) = 375 mL
16 fluid ounces (2 cups) = 500 mL

WEIGHTS (mass)

1/2 ounce = 15 g
1 ounce = 30 g
3 ounces = 90 g
4 ounces = 120 g
8 ounces = 225 g
10 ounces = 285 g
12 ounces = 360 g
16 ounces = 1 pound = 450 g

DIMENSIONS

1/16 inch = 2 mm
1/8 inch = 3 mm
1/4 inch = 6 mm
1/2 inch = 1.5 cm
3/4 inch = 2 cm
1 inch = 2.5 cm

OVEN TEMPERATURES

250°F = 120°C
275°F = 140°C
300°F = 150°C
325°F = 160°C
350°F = 180°C
375°F = 190°C
400°F = 200°C
425°F = 220°C
450°F = 230°C

BAKING PAN SIZES

Utensil	Size in Inches/Quarts	Metric Volume	Size in Centimeters
Baking or Cake Pan (square or rectangular)	8×8×2	2 L	20×20×5
	9×9×2	2.5 L	23×23×5
	12×8×2	3 L	30×20×5
	13×9×2	3.5 L	33×23×5
Loaf Pan	8×4×3	1.5 L	20×10×7
	9×5×3	2 L	23×13×7
Round Layer Cake Pan	8×1½	1.2 L	20×4
	9×1½	1.5 L	23×4
Pie Plate	8×1¼	750 mL	20×3
	9×1¼	1 L	23×3
Baking Dish or Casserole	1 quart	1 L	—
	1½ quart	1.5 L	—
	2 quart	2 L	—